The **ADHD RSD Workbook** is an in-depth resource crafted to offer a comprehensive understanding of Rejection Sensitive Dysphoria (RSD) and its connection to Attention Deficit Hyperactivity Disorder (ADHD). This workbook delves into the intricate nature of RSD, explaining its characteristics, the neurological basis behind it, and how it intertwines with ADHD.

The workbook begins by introducing RSD, defining its core aspects, and exploring the emotional impact it has on individuals. It explains how RSD is a neurological phenomenon, detailing how various brain regions, such as the limbic system and prefrontal cortex, contribute to the intensity of emotional responses experienced during RSD episodes. The role of neurochemicals like dopamine in regulating these emotions is also examined.

Further, the workbook provides a vivid portrayal of what an RSD episode feels like, from subtle emotional reactions to severe breakdowns. It outlines how these experiences can vary in intensity and how they impact self-esteem, confidence, and overall psychological well-being. The text also connects RSD to broader issues like anxiety and depression, highlighting the long-term psychological effects of repeated RSD episodes.

In addition to understanding RSD, the workbook offers practical strategies for managing it. It includes cognitive behavioral therapy (CBT) exercises, emphasizes the importance of journaling, and provides affirmations to support emotional regulation before, during, and after RSD episodes. To build self-awareness, the workbook features a personality assessment tailored to ADHD and

RSD, along with exercises designed to improve emotional control and self-awareness.

The workbook also addresses the concept of emotional safety, explaining why rejection can feel like a significant threat and offering coping mechanisms to create a sense of emotional security. It concludes by encouraging patience and persistence in managing RSD and provides resources and support options for ongoing assistance.

Overall, the **ADHD RSD Workbook** is a thorough guide designed to help individuals understand and navigate the challenges of Rejection Sensitive Dysphoria, fostering greater emotional resilience and self-awareness in the context of ADHD.

The Impact of Rejection and RSD

RSD can make any form of rejection, especially from someone as significant as a parent, feel deeply painful. When someone close, like your mother, rejects you, it can feel like an attack on your entire sense of self-worth. People with RSD often feel the rejection as if it's their fault, or they believe it validates every fear they've ever had about not being good enough. Even though that rejection isn't about who you are as a person, it can feel intensely personal, and it can leave emotional scars that are hard to shake.

- **Why you're experiencing this:** When someone with ADHD and RSD experiences rejection, the emotional brain takes over. You may constantly replay the event in your mind, leading to feelings of worthlessness and shame. It can feel like a confirmation of your deepest fears—that you're not lovable or deserving of a healthy relationship. These feelings can also linger and feed into depression, causing you to spiral into self-blame and anxiety.

2. Low Self-Esteem and Identity

With the rejection from your mother and your ongoing struggle with RSD, it's likely that your self-esteem has taken a significant hit. ADHD itself can make it hard to maintain a positive sense of self because it often brings feelings of failure from unmet expectations or not being able to keep up with others. RSD intensifies this by making you hyper-sensitive to negative feedback, both real and perceived.

Now, combine that with a significant rejection from someone as influential as a parent, and it's easy to see why your self-esteem may feel shattered. When you don't feel good about yourself, everything around you—like social situations, meeting new people, or even leaving the house—can trigger anxiety.

- **Why you're experiencing this:** Your mother's rejection might feel like a reflection of your worth. With ADHD and RSD, it becomes even harder to shake these feelings because your brain tends to focus on the emotional pain. It's natural to avoid situations where you fear more rejection or judgment, like meeting your husband's clients. The idea of facing others might feel like another chance for someone to hurt or judge you, which feeds into the anxiety you're feeling.

3. Depression and Anxiety

Depression and anxiety often go hand in hand, particularly when dealing with ADHD and RSD. Depression can stem from a long history of feeling like you're not measuring up or that you're constantly being rejected, whether socially, professionally, or by loved ones. Anxiety, on the other hand, often arises from the fear of future rejection or failure, especially in social or high-pressure situations.

Your anxiety about leaving the house or meeting new people might come from this overwhelming fear of being judged or rejected again. This creates a cycle where your anxiety feeds your depression, which then makes it even harder to break out of these patterns. The thought of facing people who don't know what you're going through can feel paralyzing, as you anticipate their judgment or disapproval.

- **Why you're experiencing this:** The fear of meeting new people or stepping outside could be rooted in the belief that you're not good enough or that people will see your struggles and judge you. Depression can also make you feel like nothing you do will make things better, so it becomes difficult to motivate yourself to engage with the outside world.

4. Emotional Paralysis from RSD

When RSD episodes occur, they often cause a form of emotional paralysis. It's not just about feeling sad or anxious, but about feeling stuck—unable to move forward because of the weight of all the negative emotions you're carrying. With RSD, rejection feels deeply personal, and even the *thought* of future rejection can cause anxiety to spike, which may be why you feel such intense discomfort at the idea of meeting your husband's clients.

- **Why you're experiencing this:** Your brain is wired to feel emotional pain intensely, so rejection or the anticipation of it makes you feel completely overwhelmed. This can create a sort of avoidance behavior, where you might want to avoid social interactions or new situations because of the fear of being judged or misunderstood.

5. Unresolved Grief and Family Rejection

When a parent rejects you, it's one of the deepest emotional wounds a person can experience. Your relationship with your mother may have been a significant source of self-identity, and her rejection may feel like a deep loss, even if the relationship was strained.

This unresolved grief can linger and affect how you view yourself and your other relationships. You might feel like you're unworthy of love or acceptance, which can affect how you interact with others, like your husband's clients. This grief can manifest as anxiety, making you feel more vulnerable and emotionally fragile.

- **Why you're experiencing this:** Family rejection can make you question your inherent value, leaving you with a sense of emptiness. It can trigger a belief that if your own mother rejected you, others might too, which leads to anxiety about facing the world.

Ways to Begin Healing:

1. **Acknowledge your feelings:** It's important to validate your emotions. You've experienced deep pain and rejection, and that's hard. Allow yourself to grieve and express what you're feeling, even if it's through journaling or talking with someone you trust.

2. **Therapy:** Cognitive Behavioral Therapy (CBT) is effective for dealing with RSD, anxiety, and depression. A therapist can help you work through the root causes of your emotions and develop strategies for managing them.

3. **Start small with exposure:** If meeting clients feels overwhelming, start by setting small, achievable goals for leaving the house or interacting with others. Gradual exposure to these anxiety-provoking situations can help reduce their power over time.

4. **Challenge your thoughts:** RSD and anxiety often cause you to catastrophize or think in black-and-

white terms. Challenge these thoughts by asking yourself if they're really true. Remind yourself that others' opinions don't define your worth.

5. **Rebuild self-esteem:** Focus on small wins and things you enjoy doing. Celebrating these small victories can help slowly build your confidence.

6. **Seek support:** You don't have to go through this alone. Whether it's friends, family, or a support group, connecting with others who understand your experiences can help you feel less isolated.

Emotional Response Assessment

The Emotional Response Assessment is a tool designed to help individuals explore and differentiate their reactions to rejection and criticism. It focuses on identifying four distinct types of emotional responses: Typical Emotional Responses to Rejection, Heightened Emotional Sensitivity, Perceived Sensitivity to Criticism (sometimes colloquially referred to as "snowflake" behavior), and Rejection Sensitive Dysphoria (RSD).

This assessment is crucial because it provides insight into the various ways people handle rejection and criticism, offering clarity on where one's reactions might fall on a spectrum. Understanding these responses is essential for developing effective coping strategies and managing emotional reactions more effectively.

It is important to note that this assessment is not a diagnostic tool. While it can provide valuable information about emotional patterns and sensitivities, it is not intended to diagnose any conditions or disorders. The responses identified through the assessment may overlap with or be mistaken for other emotional or psychological issues, making it essential to consider them within the broader context of one's overall mental health.

By distinguishing between typical reactions, heightened sensitivity, perceived sensitivity, and RSD, individuals can gain a better understanding of their emotional responses. This awareness can guide them toward appropriate strategies for managing their emotions and seeking the right type of support. The assessment serves as a starting point for self-reflection and emotional management, rather than a definitive diagnosis or a replacement for professional mental health evaluation.

Introduction to the Assessment

Welcome to the **Emotional Response Assessment**. This tool is designed to help you understand and differentiate between various emotional reactions to rejection and criticism. By exploring your responses to these experiences, you can gain valuable insights into your emotional patterns and how they impact your well-being.

Purpose of the Assessment

The purpose of this assessment is to:

1. **Identify and Differentiate Emotional Responses:** The assessment covers four key areas: Typical Emotional Responses to Rejection, Heightened Emotional Sensitivity, Perceived Sensitivity to Criticism (sometimes colloquially referred to as "snowflake" behavior), and Rejection Sensitive Dysphoria (RSD). Understanding these distinctions can help you identify which category best describes your experiences.

2. **Promote Self-Awareness:** By reflecting on your emotional reactions, you can develop a clearer understanding of how you handle rejection and criticism. This self-awareness is crucial for recognizing patterns in your behavior and emotional responses.

3. **Enhance Emotional Regulation:** Knowing whether you experience typical, heightened, or dysphoric responses to rejection can guide you in adopting appropriate coping strategies. This insight can help you manage your emotions more effectively and reduce unnecessary distress.

4. **Facilitate Personal Growth:** Understanding your emotional responses allows you to address specific areas where you may need support or development. Whether it's improving resilience, managing sensitivity, or addressing RSD, this assessment can be a valuable tool for personal growth.

Importance of Self-Awareness

Self-awareness is a key component of emotional intelligence and personal development. Knowing the difference between typical emotional responses, heightened sensitivity, perceived sensitivity, and RSD is important for several reasons:

1. **Improved Emotional Management:** Recognizing where your reactions fall on the spectrum allows you to choose the most effective strategies for managing your emotions. For example, if you identify as having RSD, you may benefit from specialized coping techniques or professional support.

2. **Better Interpersonal Relationships:** Understanding your emotional responses helps you communicate more effectively with others and manage conflicts constructively. It can also enhance your empathy and improve your relationships by providing insight into how others may perceive and respond to your reactions.

3. **Enhanced Self-Compassion:** By acknowledging and understanding your emotional patterns, you can develop a kinder, more compassionate approach to yourself. This self-compassion is essential for maintaining mental well-being and fostering a positive self-image.

4. **Targeted Support and Interventions:** Differentiating between these emotional responses enables you to seek targeted support, whether it's through therapy, self-help strategies, or other resources. It ensures

that you receive the right kind of help to address your specific needs.

Overall, this assessment is designed to provide you with a deeper understanding of your emotional responses and to guide you toward more effective strategies for managing rejection and criticism. Your journey toward greater self-awareness is a crucial step in achieving emotional balance and personal growth.

Normal Reaction to Rejection

- **Typical Emotional Response to Rejection**: This term reflects a standard or expected emotional reaction when facing rejection or criticism. It represents a healthy level of resilience where the individual can handle rejection without excessive distress.

Being Sensitive

- **Heightened Emotional Sensitivity**: This term describes an increased responsiveness to emotional stimuli or feedback. It implies that the person is more affected by rejection or criticism than average but does not necessarily mean they have a clinical condition.

Snowflake (Perceived as Looking for Conflict)

- **Perceived Sensitivity to Criticism**: This term addresses the perception that someone is overly sensitive or prone to taking offense. It captures the idea that the individual may react strongly to perceived slights or conflicts, whether or not these reactions are proportionate.

Rejection Sensitive Dysphoria (RSD)

- **Rejection Sensitive Dysphoria (RSD)**: This term accurately describes a condition characterized by intense emotional pain and distress in response to rejection or criticism. RSD is often associated with ADHD and involves severe emotional and sometimes physical reactions to perceived or actual rejection.

QUESTIONS

General Emotional Responses

1. How do you typically respond when someone gives you constructive criticism?
2. Do you feel rejected even when the rejection isn't personal?
3. How long do you usually feel upset after receiving negative feedback?

4. Do you ever feel like you're overreacting to minor criticism?

5. What kind of thoughts run through your mind after someone criticizes or rejects you?

6. Are you more sensitive to rejection from people you're close to, or does it hurt equally from anyone?

7. Can you bounce back from rejection quickly, or does it affect you for an extended period?

8. Do you often feel that people are out to hurt your feelings intentionally?

9. Do you spend a lot of time replaying rejection or criticism in your head, even if it's minor?

10. How often do you seek reassurance from others after feeling criticized or rejected?

Sensitivity to Rejection

1. How do you feel when someone disagrees with your opinion?

2. Do you often feel misunderstood in social situations?

3. Do you find yourself getting defensive when someone offers advice or feedback?

4. When rejected, do you immediately question your self-worth or abilities?

5. How likely are you to internalize other people's opinions of you?

6. Do you tend to avoid situations where you might be rejected or criticized?

7. How often do you take neutral or casual remarks as personal insults?

8. Do you feel like you need validation from others to feel okay about yourself?

9. Are there specific types of rejection or criticism that hurt you more than others?

10. Do you avoid social interactions because you fear people won't like or accept you?

Emotional Regulation and Self-Control

1. How well can you control your emotions when facing rejection or criticism?

2. Do you feel out of control when you're upset after being rejected?

3. How do you calm yourself down after experiencing rejection or criticism?

4. Do you tend to lash out at others when you feel rejected or hurt?

5. Do you feel an intense emotional reaction when someone disagrees with you?

6. Are you able to separate someone's rejection of your ideas from a rejection of you as a person?

7. When someone criticizes you, do you immediately assume it's a reflection of your worth?

8. How often do you allow rejection to affect your day-to-day mood or actions?

9. Do you find it difficult to concentrate or function after being rejected or criticized?

10. How do you handle situations where people don't give you the response you were hoping for?

Perception of Self-Worth

1. How do you typically feel about yourself when you're not receiving external validation?

2. Do you believe your self-worth depends on what others think of you?

3. Do you tend to take rejection as proof that you're not good enough?

4. When you experience rejection, do you feel like you've failed as a person?

5. How do you define your self-worth? Is it mostly based on your actions or how others view you?

6. Does rejection make you question your abilities or intelligence?

7. How do you feel about yourself after a positive interaction versus after a rejection?
8. Can you maintain a stable sense of self-worth even after being rejected?
9. How much importance do you place on the opinions of others?
10. Do you feel like you have to be perfect to be worthy of love or acceptance?

Sensitivity or Looking for Conflict (Perceived "Snowflake" Behavior)

1. How often do you feel offended by comments or jokes that others consider harmless?
2. Do you frequently believe that people are being intentionally mean or dismissive towards you?
3. Do you often find yourself getting angry at things others seem unaffected by?
4. When you're upset, do you feel that others are always to blame for your emotions?
5. Do you feel like you have to correct people or call them out when they say something you disagree with?
6. Do you often feel like people are "walking on eggshells" around you to avoid upsetting you?

7. How often do you believe that people are unfair or unjust towards you?

8. Do you find it hard to let go of situations where you felt wronged or insulted?

9. Do you often assume that people are trying to hurt your feelings intentionally?

10. Are you more likely to assume someone meant harm even if they clarify they didn't?

Identifying Average Rejection

1. How often do you experience everyday rejections (e.g., someone not texting back)?

2. Can you differentiate between personal and impersonal forms of rejection?

3. Do you often feel like small rejections are much bigger deals than others do?

4. Are you able to see someone's criticism or rejection as unrelated to your overall value?

5. How well do you handle everyday challenges like not being invited to a party or not getting a job?

6. Are you able to accept that rejection is a part of life, or do you struggle with it deeply?

7. How often do you let small rejections affect your whole mood or outlook?

8. When rejected, do you assume there's something wrong with you personally, or do you view it as situational?
9. How do you feel about rejection when it's constructive (e.g., in a work or school setting)?
10. Can you put a rejection into perspective and move forward without dwelling on it?

Distinguishing RSD (Rejection Sensitive Dysphoria)

1. How intense is your emotional reaction to rejection or criticism, compared to others around you?
2. Do you experience physical symptoms (e.g., heart racing, shaking) when you feel rejected?
3. How long do you dwell on feelings of rejection? Is it hours, days, or longer?
4. Do you feel as though even minor rejections can cause extreme emotional pain?
5. Do you tend to overthink situations where you feel like you've been rejected, replaying them in your head?
6. Does rejection feel unbearable to the point where it's hard to function afterward?

7. How often do you avoid situations that could lead to rejection due to fear of intense emotional pain?

8. When someone doesn't respond the way you expected, do you assume they're rejecting you?

9. How often does your fear of rejection prevent you from taking risks or trying new things?

10. When rejected, do you experience thoughts that are overly negative or catastrophic?

Navigating Criticism

1. How do you feel when someone offers you constructive feedback? Do you take it personally?

2. Do you ever feel personally attacked even when someone is trying to help you improve?

3. How often do you react defensively to even mild forms of criticism?

4. Do you tend to hear criticism even in situations where none was intended?

5. Can you differentiate between someone's opinion and a direct critique of who you are?

6. How do you handle criticism that comes from someone you respect or care about?

7. How often do you interpret neutral comments as criticism or rejection?

8. When criticized, do you immediately question your value or self-worth?

9. How do you handle rejection from someone you don't know well versus someone close to you?

10. How do you feel when someone points out a mistake you made, even if they're kind about it?

Managing Emotional Reactions

1. How well can you reflect on your emotions after the initial rejection? Can you think about it calmly?

2. Do you ever feel overwhelmed by your emotions to the point where you can't control your reaction?

3. Are you prone to emotional outbursts when feeling criticized or rejected?

4. When someone criticizes you, do you find it difficult to think rationally afterward?

5. Do your emotions feel out of proportion to the situation when you're rejected?

6. How often do you cry, feel angry, or feel physically ill after being rejected?

7. Do you feel ashamed of how intensely you react to rejection or criticism?

8. How often do you regret your reaction after calming down from being rejected?

9. How likely are you to ruminate on your emotional pain for days or even weeks?

10. Do you experience emotional highs and lows depending on how others treat you?

Understanding Emotional Triggers

1. Can you identify specific triggers that make rejection feel unbearable to you?

2. Do certain people or situations make you more prone to feeling rejected?

3. How do you feel when people don't meet your expectations (e.g., not responding to a text)?

4. What situations make you feel most vulnerable to rejection?

5. How often do you feel rejected when others don't offer you immediate validation?

6. Do certain phrases or actions from others automatically make you feel rejected?

7. Can you separate your emotions from what's actually happening in a situation?

8. Do you feel triggered by rejection or criticism more in certain environments (e.g., work vs. personal)?

9. How do you handle rejection when it comes from people you care about versus strangers?

10. Are you aware of how past rejections may affect your current emotional responses?

Table of Contents for ADHD RSD Workbook

1. **Introduction to Rejection Sensitive Dysphoria (RSD)**
   - What is RSD?
   - The Connection Between ADHD and RSD
   - Understanding the Emotional Impact of RSD

1. **RSD: A Brain Thing**
   - How RSD is Wired in the Brain
   - The Role of the Limbic System in Emotional Responses
   - Neurochemical Factors: Dopamine and Emotional Regulation
   - Why Logic Doesn't Always Help: The Prefrontal Cortex and Emotional Control

1. **The Experience of an RSD Episode**
   - Signs of an RSD Episode: How to Recognize It
   - Why It Feels Uncontrollable: The Automatic Emotional Response
   - The Emotional Breakdown: What It Feels Like in the Moment

1. **Different Degrees of RSD: From Moderate to Severe**
   - Moderate RSD: Subtle Reactions and Emotional Sensitivity
   - Severe RSD: Overwhelming Emotional Breakdown
   - How RSD Can Vary in Intensity
1. **Understanding the Impact of RSD on Self-Esteem**
   - How RSD Affects Self-Worth and Confidence
   - Why Negative Comments Can Shatter Self-Esteem
   - The Link Between RSD, Anxiety, and Depression
1. **Navigating Self-Esteem with ADHD and RSD**
   - Why Self-Esteem is Fragile in ADHD
   - Strategies for Building and Maintaining Steady Self-Esteem
   - Affirmations to Support Self-Esteem Before, During, and After RSD Episodes
1. **The Psychological Toll of RSD**
   - Long-Term Psychological Damage from RSD
   - How Repeated Episodes Affect Mental Health
   - The Role of Rejection in Anxiety and Depression
1. **Coping with RSD: Tools and Techniques**
   - Cognitive Behavioral Therapy (CBT) Exercises for RSD
   - The Importance of Journaling in Managing RSD

1. **Conclusion**
   - Understanding the Complexity of RSD
   - The Road to Managing RSD: Patience and Persistence
   - Finding Support and Resources for ADHD and RSD

Rejection Sensitive Dysphoria (RSD): A More Accurate Description

Rejection Sensitive Dysphoria (RSD) is a condition that affects people with ADHD (Attention Deficit Hyperactivity Disorder) and other neurodiverse individuals. It's characterized by an extreme emotional response to perceived or actual criticism, rejection, or failure. For someone with RSD, these feelings of rejection or disapproval aren't just uncomfortable; they are devastating and all-consuming, often leading to emotional outbursts or internalized pain.

RSD can manifest quickly, with emotions hitting intensely and often without warning. The severity of the emotional reaction is disproportionate to the situation, but for the person experiencing it, the feelings are real and overwhelming.

Rejection Sensitive Dysphoria (RSD) has not been fully addressed or recognized in the medical community for several reasons:

Complexity and Overlap

RSD is a complex emotional phenomenon that overlaps with other psychological conditions and symptoms, making it challenging to categorize distinctly. It involves intense emotional responses to perceived rejection or criticism, which can be similar to symptoms of other disorders such as anxiety, depression, and mood disorders. This overlap complicates efforts to isolate and define RSD as a standalone condition, leading to its treatment being incorporated into broader ADHD management strategies rather than being recognized independently.

Lack of Formal Research

One significant reason for the lack of recognition is the limited amount of formal research on RSD. While RSD is widely acknowledged within the ADHD community, it has not been extensively studied in clinical settings or incorporated into large-scale research projects. This lack of empirical data contributes to its absence in major diagnostic manuals like the DSM-5, which relies on substantial research and clinical evidence for the inclusion of conditions.

Diagnostic Criteria and Frameworks

The DSM-5 and other diagnostic frameworks are developed based on extensive clinical trials and research, and they use specific criteria for diagnosing mental health conditions. RSD, while a well-documented experience among individuals with ADHD, does not yet meet the rigorous criteria required for inclusion in these diagnostic manuals. The focus on more universally recognized conditions often means that less understood or less common symptoms, like RSD, may not receive the same level of attention or formal recognition.

Variability in Symptoms

RSD manifests differently in each individual, with a wide range of symptoms and triggers. This variability can make it challenging to create a standardized definition or treatment protocol. Because RSD symptoms can vary significantly, it is difficult for the medical community to develop a uniform approach to diagnosing and managing it.

Advocacy and Awareness

Within the ADHD community, there is growing advocacy for recognizing and addressing RSD, but this awareness has not yet translated into widespread formal acknowledgment in the broader medical field. As the understanding of RSD continues to evolve, increased advocacy, research, and clinical evidence will be crucial in pushing for its formal recognition and integration into standard diagnostic and treatment practices.

Evolving Knowledge

The field of psychology and psychiatry is continually evolving, and new understandings and conditions are regularly being explored. As awareness of RSD grows and more research is conducted, there is potential for it to gain formal recognition in the future. However, until there is substantial research and evidence supporting its distinct status, it remains an area of interest primarily within the ADHD community rather than mainstream medical practice.

In summary, the lack of recognition for RSD in the medical community is due to its complex nature, overlap with other conditions, limited formal research, variability in symptoms, and evolving knowledge within the field. Increasing awareness and research are essential steps toward gaining formal acknowledgment and developing effective treatments for RSD.

Signs of an RSD Episode

An RSD episode can present in various ways, depending on the individual and their personal triggers. Here are common signs:

1. **Intense Emotional Distress:** A sudden flood of emotions — typically sadness, anger, or fear — overwhelms the person, often accompanied by a sense of hopelessness or worthlessness.

2. **Hyper-Sensitivity to Criticism or Rejection:** Even minor feedback or an offhand remark can feel like a deep personal attack. The person may feel as though their entire self-worth is being questioned.

3. **Irritability or Anger Outbursts:** When the emotions become too overwhelming, they may express them outwardly through anger or irritability, sometimes directed at others who had no involvement in the triggering event.

4. **Withdrawal or Social Avoidance:** To avoid further pain or rejection, the person may withdraw from social situations, isolating themselves. This can sometimes result in feelings of loneliness and disconnection.

5. **Low Self-Esteem or Self-Deprecation:** The person may internalize the criticism or rejection, believing they are inherently flawed or unworthy. These negative self-perceptions can persist long after the episode ends.

6. **Physical Symptoms:** Some individuals experience physical symptoms during an RSD episode, such as stomachaches, headaches, or a feeling of nausea due to the intense emotional and psychological distress.

7. **Panic or Anxiety:** The fear of being rejected or criticized can also lead to anxiety or panic attacks, particularly when anticipating situations where they might face judgment.

Degrees of Emotional Impact

RSD doesn't affect everyone in the same way, and the degree of emotional impact can vary greatly based on factors like individual resilience, environmental context, and past experiences. Below are the different degrees of emotional impact:

1. Moderate Emotional Impact:

- **Description:** In moderate cases, the person may feel hurt by criticism or rejection, but they are still able to cope with the feelings. They may feel down for a few hours or days, but they can process the emotions and bounce back relatively quickly.
- **Emotional Response:** Mild sadness, slight anxiety, or temporary irritation. These emotions, though painful, do not completely overwhelm the person.
- **Effect on Behavior:** The person might ruminate on the perceived rejection or criticism but can move on without it significantly affecting their day-to-day life.

2. Significant Emotional Impact:

- **Description:** In cases with significant emotional impact, the person feels more deeply hurt, and the emotional fallout lasts longer. They may feel that their self-worth is being questioned and find it difficult to move past the situation.
- **Emotional Response:** Intense sadness, feelings of worthlessness, and bouts of anger or frustration. They might feel anxious about future social situations.
- **Effect on Behavior:** This level of RSD may lead to avoidance behaviors, such as withdrawing from social situations or procrastinating on tasks that involve potential feedback or criticism. The person may have trouble focusing on other aspects of their life while ruminating on the rejection.

3. Severe Emotional Impact:

- **Description:** In severe cases, RSD can lead to overwhelming feelings of shame, embarrassment, or self-hatred. The person feels as though the rejection defines their entire self-worth, and these feelings are deeply distressing.
- **Emotional Response:** Overwhelming, uncontrollable emotions. This might manifest in crying, panic attacks,

intense anger, or even self-harm ideation. The emotional pain is so severe that the person feels consumed by it.

- **Effect on Behavior:** At this stage, the person may shut down emotionally or socially, avoiding situations that might trigger RSD. This could lead to isolation, anxiety, and depression. They may struggle to function in work or relationships because the emotional toll is so high.

Psychological Damage Caused by RSD

When RSD episodes occur frequently or severely, the long-term psychological damage can be significant. Here are the potential consequences:

1. Chronic Low Self-Esteem:

People with RSD may constantly feel inadequate or unworthy because of the intense emotional reactions they experience to even minor criticisms. Over time, they may begin to believe that they are inherently flawed, leading to chronic low self-esteem.

2. Social Anxiety and Avoidance:

RSD can lead to avoidance of social interactions, especially those that involve potential criticism or feedback. This can evolve into social anxiety, where the person feels overwhelming fear in social situations, particularly if they believe they are at risk of being judged or rejected.

3. **Perfectionism and Fear of Failure:**

To avoid triggering an RSD episode, some people become perfectionists. They may place enormous pressure on themselves to never make mistakes or to constantly seek approval, which can lead to burnout and increased stress. The fear of failure becomes paralyzing, as they associate any failure with personal rejection.

4. **Emotional Dysregulation:**

RSD episodes can lead to difficulties in emotional regulation. The person may find it difficult to manage even minor emotional fluctuations, resulting in intense emotional highs and lows. This can make it hard to navigate relationships, careers, and other aspects of life.

5. **Depression and Anxiety:**

Long-term RSD can contribute to the development of mental health conditions like depression and generalized anxiety. The constant fear of rejection and the emotional toll of RSD episodes can leave the person feeling trapped, hopeless, and exhausted.

6. **Relationship Issues:**

RSD can severely impact relationships. The person might push people away, become overly sensitive to their partner's remarks, or constantly seek reassurance. Over time, this emotional sensitivity can strain personal and professional relationships.

7. **Emotional Numbness or Disconnection:**

As a way to cope with repeated emotional breakdowns, some people may emotionally disconnect or shut down. They might distance themselves from others or become numb to protect themselves from future pain. While this can temporarily provide relief, it also limits the person's ability to connect deeply with others, further isolating them.

Rejection Sensitive Dysphoria (RSD) is a serious emotional challenge for many people with ADHD and other neurodiverse conditions. It goes far beyond typical emotional sensitivity, as the emotional reactions are immediate, intense, and feel inescapable. Whether the emotional impact is moderate or severe, RSD episodes can leave lasting psychological damage, including low self-esteem, anxiety, and relationship issues.

Understanding that RSD is *wired* into the brain can help explain why these episodes feel so uncontrollable. The emotional brain takes charge, and logic often loses its influence. It's important to recognize that while RSD cannot be completely eradicated, developing coping mechanisms and emotional regulation strategies can help those affected better manage their intense emotions.

Rejection Sensitive Dysphoria (RSD) isn't something that can be controlled consciously because it's deeply rooted in the brain's automatic response systems. It's not a matter of simply "thinking positively" or "controlling emotions" because the brain itself is wired to react intensely to perceived rejection or criticism.

Why RSD Happens Automatically in the Brain

RSD is tied to the brain's emotional regulation and response mechanisms, particularly within the **limbic system**. This part of the brain is responsible for managing our emotions, memories, and reactions to stimuli. For people with RSD, their brain interprets even small criticisms or rejections as severe emotional threats. This triggers an automatic, intense response, much like a fight-or-flight reaction to physical danger.

In people with ADHD, the connections between the emotional brain (limbic system) and the executive brain (prefrontal cortex) — the part that manages reasoning and impulse control — can be less efficient. The emotional brain reacts much faster and with more intensity, and the logical brain has a harder time stepping in to calm things down. As a result, when someone with RSD perceives rejection, the emotional part of the brain overrides the logical part, making it almost impossible to stop or control the feelings.

How the Brain Reacts in RSD

1. **Hyperactivity of Emotional Centers:** The **amygdala**, which is part of the limbic system, is responsible for emotional responses, especially fear and anxiety. In people with RSD, the amygdala becomes hyperactive in response to perceived rejection. Even the slightest

hint of criticism can trigger this part of the brain, creating an overwhelming emotional reaction.

2. **Reduced Impulse Control:** The **prefrontal cortex,** responsible for logical thinking and emotional regulation, struggles to keep up. This area of the brain is often less active or slower in people with ADHD. So, when the amygdala is firing off intense emotional responses, the prefrontal cortex can't effectively step in to dampen the reaction.

3. **Immediate, Involuntary Reaction:** The emotional response happens so quickly that it bypasses conscious control. By the time someone with RSD is aware of their feelings, the emotional brain has already taken over, creating feelings of intense sadness, anger, or panic. This is why, in the middle of an RSD episode, logic or reasoning seems ineffective — the emotional brain has completely overrun the system.

The Neurochemical Aspect

Neurotransmitters, like **dopamine** and **norepinephrine,** play a significant role in ADHD and RSD. People with ADHD typically have a dopamine deficiency, which can lead to emotional dysregulation. Since dopamine is involved in pleasure and reward pathways, a lack of it makes individuals hypersensitive to feedback. When a person with RSD perceives rejection, it can feel disproportionately negative because their brain isn't getting enough of the "feel-good" chemicals needed to balance the emotional experience.

Why It Feels Uncontrollable

The brain's emotional response during an RSD episode is not something that can be stopped once it begins. The limbic system takes control, and the brain's wiring makes it difficult to pause, reflect, and redirect the emotional reaction. This is why it can feel like the emotions are overwhelming and inescapable — because they are, in that moment, biologically wired to be overwhelming.

It's Not About Weakness or Overreacting

It's crucial to understand that RSD is not a matter of being overly sensitive or unable to "handle" emotions. The brain is literally wired in a way that amplifies the emotional impact of rejection. For people with RSD, the response is as automatic and uncontrollable as a reflex.

Trying to suppress or control an RSD episode through logic or willpower alone is often ineffective because the brain's emotional centers are already in overdrive. The key to managing RSD isn't in stopping the response from happening but in developing coping strategies to navigate it after it starts. Over time, with practice and support, people can learn how to work with their emotional responses, even if they can't stop the initial feelings.

RSD Is a "Brain Thing"

RSD is a neurological condition rooted in the brain's automatic emotional response system. It's not about choice or control, and it happens involuntarily because of how the brain processes rejection or criticism. Understanding that RSD is "wired" into the brain can help remove the stigma of "overreacting" and shift the focus to developing strategies for coping with the intense emotional waves when they come.

Rejection Sensitive Dysphoria (RSD) can manifest in varying degrees of intensity, depending on the individual and their life experiences. While RSD is a common feature for people with ADHD, its impact can range from moderate to severe, influencing both emotional responses and overall well-being. Let's explore the different levels of RSD and how it affects people.

1. **Moderate RSD**

In cases of moderate RSD, the emotional response to perceived rejection or criticism is present, but it doesn't fully consume the individual. The emotional pain is sharp and real, but it may not completely derail daily functioning. While these feelings are still intense, people with moderate RSD can often recover relatively quickly or use coping strategies to manage the distress.

Key Features of Moderate RSD:

- Frequent over-analysis of social interactions: People might replay conversations in their mind, worrying if they upset someone or were misunderstood. However, they are still able to rationalize these situations after some time.
- Emotional discomfort in response to rejection: The feelings of rejection can be painful but not all-consuming. The individual may still feel upset, but

they can process the emotions more effectively after some reflection.

- Tendency to avoid conflict: In an effort to avoid feelings of rejection, individuals might be slightly conflict-averse but can still handle difficult conversations without completely shutting down.
- Anxiety in social situations: There might be mild to moderate social anxiety, especially around people who are seen as critical. However, this anxiety isn't typically paralyzing.

Example:

Someone with moderate RSD might feel a sense of anxiety after a disagreement at work, replaying the situation in their head and wondering if their coworker now dislikes them. However, after talking it through with a trusted friend or after a night of rest, they can acknowledge that the situation wasn't as bad as it seemed and move forward.

Recovery Time:

- Recovery from rejection or perceived failure might take a few hours or up to a day, but the individual is able to regain emotional stability without it affecting their week.

2. High RSD

At this stage, high RSD involves more intense emotional reactions to perceived rejection or criticism. These emotions can last longer and be more challenging to control, often spilling over into various areas of life, such as work, relationships, and self-esteem. Individuals with high RSD can struggle to manage these feelings, and the impact on their self-image and social interactions becomes more pronounced.

Key Features of High RSD:

- Heightened sensitivity to criticism: Even mild criticism can feel devastating. The individual might take negative feedback personally, seeing it as a reflection of their worth, leading to a disproportionate emotional response.
- Emotional intensity: Emotional reactions are intense, often including feelings of humiliation, anger, or deep sadness. These emotions can feel difficult to control and overwhelming.

- Social withdrawal: Due to fear of rejection or failure, people with high RSD might avoid situations that could potentially lead to criticism, such as challenging social settings, work projects, or even intimate relationships.
- Overwhelming self-doubt: High RSD can fuel self-esteem issues, making individuals question their value and abilities. They may feel as though they are constantly failing, even if they are performing well.

Example:

After receiving constructive criticism from a supervisor, a person with high RSD might feel devastated and assume they are going to lose their job. They may ruminate on the feedback for days, even if the feedback was neutral or helpful. The emotional fallout can extend beyond work, making them feel anxious in other areas of life.

Recovery Time:

- Recovery might take several days, and it can be difficult to bounce back. Emotions linger longer, and it can affect mood, motivation, and confidence for extended periods.

3. Severe RSD

Severe RSD involves an extreme and sometimes paralyzing reaction to perceived rejection or criticism. The emotional pain can be overwhelming, and it's common for individuals with severe RSD to experience long-lasting effects from these episodes. This level of RSD can significantly interfere with daily life, often leading to avoidance of social situations, withdrawal from relationships, and even intense emotional breakdowns. Severe RSD can also contribute to mental health conditions such as anxiety, depression, and suicidal ideation.

Key Features of Severe RSD:

- **Extreme emotional responses:** Individuals experience intense emotional pain, humiliation, anger, or sadness in response to perceived rejection. The reaction feels overwhelming, often leading to emotional breakdowns or outbursts.
- **Hypervigilance to rejection:** People with severe RSD are constantly on edge, expecting criticism or rejection even when it's not present. They might misinterpret neutral interactions as negative or hostile.

- **Difficulty regulating emotions:** Severe RSD makes it nearly impossible to control emotional responses. Logic and reasoning seem irrelevant when in the midst of an RSD episode, and individuals may feel consumed by their feelings of rejection.
- **Avoidance and withdrawal:** To protect themselves from further emotional pain, individuals may start to isolate themselves socially, avoiding any situation that could result in rejection or failure. This can lead to loneliness, further damaging their self-esteem.
- **Self-destructive thoughts:** Severe RSD can lead to thoughts of worthlessness or hopelessness, and in some cases, suicidal ideation. The individual may feel as though they are constantly failing, regardless of objective success.

Example:

If someone with severe RSD faces even mild criticism from a friend, they might experience an immediate sense of despair, believing that they are unlovable or that their friend no longer cares for them. The emotional fallout could last for weeks, leading them to avoid social situations entirely and feel intense self-loathing.

Recovery Time:

- Recovery can take weeks or longer, depending on the severity of the RSD episode. These episodes can severely impact self-esteem, relationships, and overall quality of life.

Why RSD is So Difficult to Manage:

RSD is difficult to control because it's wired into the emotional brain, particularly in people with ADHD. When rejection is perceived, the emotional regulation systems in the brain (especially the amygdala, responsible for processing emotional responses) go into overdrive, creating an overwhelming feeling of distress. The logical part of the brain (the prefrontal cortex) is often overridden, leaving the person unable to rationalize or calm themselves down in the moment.

The nature of RSD also makes it difficult to break free from this emotional cycle because the reactions feel so immediate and personal. It often feels like rejection confirms deep-seated fears about one's self-worth.

Grading the Levels of RSD:

- **Moderate RSD:** Emotional reactions are intense but manageable. Recovery time is shorter, and individuals can use coping strategies like self-reflection or support from others to regain control.

- **High RSD:** Emotional responses are more severe and take longer to recover from. It significantly impacts relationships, self-esteem, and motivation, making it difficult to engage in social situations or handle criticism.
- **Severe RSD:** Emotional breakdowns are common, and the reaction to perceived rejection is paralyzing. Recovery can take a long time, and the emotional toll is overwhelming. Individuals often struggle with long-term emotional and psychological consequences.

RSD exists on a spectrum, from moderate to severe, and the level of intensity can change depending on the individual, their coping strategies, and life circumstances. Understanding the different levels can help people with ADHD and RSD navigate their emotions more effectively and seek appropriate support based on their experiences. Managing RSD is challenging, but with time, self-awareness, and therapeutic interventions like CBT, emotional regulation can improve.

The Role of ADHD in RSD

ADHD plays a significant role in amplifying emotional responses because of how the brain processes and manages emotions. People with ADHD often struggle with emotional self-regulation, meaning they have difficulty modulating their emotional responses to various stimuli. This can make them more vulnerable to emotional swings, particularly in response to social feedback.

Executive dysfunction, a key feature of ADHD, also contributes to RSD. Executive functions help regulate emotional responses, but individuals with ADHD may have difficulty activating the cognitive skills needed to assess the reality of a situation. This means that even a small critique can feel like a devastating blow, causing the brain to react in ways that seem disproportionate to those who do not have ADHD.

Furthermore, ADHD often involves issues with working memory. This can mean that in moments of emotional overwhelm, an individual might be unable to recall previous instances of success or affirmation, further heightening the intensity of rejection or criticism.

The issue with working memory in ADHD plays a significant role in how individuals with ADHD respond to emotional experiences, particularly during moments of emotional overwhelm. Working memory refers to the brain's ability to temporarily hold and manipulate information. For someone with ADHD, working memory tends to be impaired, which can make it harder to manage complex cognitive tasks like recalling important details, especially in emotionally charged situations.

When an individual with ADHD experiences emotional overwhelm, such as during perceived rejection or criticism, several things happen in the brain that contribute to their heightened emotional response:

1. **Working Memory Disruption in Emotional Situations**

During moments of emotional stress, working memory tends to falter, which means that the brain struggles to hold onto and recall information that could help regulate the situation. For example, when someone feels criticized, they may find it difficult to remember past instances of success or positive feedback. This is because emotional arousal, particularly in situations involving fear of rejection, can override the brain's ability to access memories that provide emotional balance or reassurance.

Without the ability to recall these positive experiences or affirmations, the person feels as though the rejection or criticism is not only accurate but also indicative of their worth or identity. The emotional intensity becomes much greater because they are "stuck" in that moment, unable to tap into memories that might soften the blow.

2. Impaired Emotional Regulation

Working memory is closely tied to executive functions, which include the ability to regulate emotions. In people with ADHD, executive dysfunction means that emotional responses are harder to control. When criticism or rejection occurs, the brain may focus intensely on that negative event, creating a sort of mental tunnel vision. In this state, the individual's working memory fails to call up examples of past achievements or moments of validation that could counterbalance the negative emotions.

In contrast, people without ADHD might automatically recall moments when they were praised or reassured, which helps them put criticism into perspective. But for someone with ADHD, this cognitive ability is often compromised during emotional stress, leading to an amplified, sometimes irrational, emotional reaction.

3. Heightened Sensitivity to Rejection

People with ADHD often have heightened emotional sensitivity, especially to perceived rejection or criticism. When working memory is impaired in moments of emotional overwhelm, this sensitivity can escalate the emotional response. Since the person is unable to remind themselves of their previous successes, they may feel like the rejection defines them or is a pattern they cannot escape. The inability to balance negative feedback with positive memories reinforces a sense of failure or inadequacy.

The intensity of Rejection Sensitive Dysphoria (RSD) in these moments is partly due to this working memory impairment. The brain simply can't access the information it needs to modulate the emotional experience, making the feelings of rejection feel overwhelming and catastrophic.

4. Cognitive Overload

ADHD brains are prone to cognitive overload, especially when managing multiple stimuli at once. In moments of emotional intensity, such as when receiving criticism, the brain is overwhelmed with processing the emotional reaction. This overload makes it even harder to access the working memory functions that could otherwise provide emotional stability. As a result, the person gets stuck in the "heat of the moment" without the ability to zoom out and remember past successes or reassuring experiences that could provide a more balanced view.

5. Fight-or-Flight Response

Emotional overwhelm can also trigger the fight-or-flight response, which is the body's natural reaction to perceived threats. For people with ADHD, criticism or rejection can feel like a personal threat. When this response is activated, the brain diverts resources away from higher-order cognitive functions, including working memory. This biological response prioritizes immediate survival over reflective thinking, making it harder to access past memories or reason through the situation.

Why Does This Make Rejection Worse?

- Inability to Self-Soothe: Without access to positive memories, the person cannot internally reassure themselves that they are capable or valued. This lack of self-soothing creates a feedback loop of negative emotions.

- Distorted Perception: Since they can't remember positive experiences, the rejection or criticism feels like the only truth. This leads to a distorted perception of reality, where the individual believes they are constantly failing or being rejected.

- RSD Amplification: For those with Rejection Sensitive Dysphoria, working memory issues heighten the intensity of rejection, as the brain can't bring forth emotional context to soften the perceived slight. Every instance of rejection feels monumental, and the pain is amplified by the inability to access emotional buffers.

In moments of emotional overwhelm, the brain's working memory in individuals with ADHD is compromised, making it difficult to recall positive experiences that could help counterbalance the immediate negative feelings. This contributes to the heightened intensity of emotional reactions in ADHD, particularly in situations involving rejection or criticism. The inability to access these past affirmations or successes means the person feels the rejection more acutely, without the cognitive resources needed to regulate their emotions or see the situation in a broader, more balanced context. Understanding this link between working memory and emotional regulation can help individuals with ADHD develop strategies to manage their emotional responses and reduce the intensity of RSD.

ADHD Impact on Self-Esteem

ADHD (Attention-Deficit/Hyperactivity Disorder) often develop low self-esteem due to the long-term challenges they face in managing their symptoms in a world that doesn't always understand or accommodate their needs. ADHD can impact various aspects of life, from academics and work to relationships and self-perception. Over time, these difficulties can contribute to a negative self-image, causing many individuals with ADHD to struggle with feelings of inadequacy, shame, and low self-worth.

Key Factors Contributing to Low Self-Esteem in Adults with ADHD

1. **Chronic Underachievement and Unrealized Potential**

Many adults with ADHD feel that they are not living up to their potential. Even if they have talent or intelligence, difficulties with focus, organization, time management, and impulsivity can prevent them from reaching their goals. Society often measures success by achievement and productivity, and when people with ADHD fail to meet these expectations, they may internalize this as personal failure rather than recognizing it as a consequence of their condition.

- **Example**: A person with ADHD might struggle to meet deadlines at work, even though they have the skills and knowledge to perform well. Repeatedly falling short of expectations can lead to a sense of incompetence and inadequacy.

2. Negative Feedback and Criticism

From a young age, individuals with ADHD are more likely to receive negative feedback from teachers, parents, peers, and employers. They may be labeled as lazy, careless, disorganized, or irresponsible. Over time, this external criticism can shape their internal dialogue, making them more likely to doubt their abilities and question their worth.

- **Example**: A child who frequently hears "You're not trying hard enough" or "You're always making careless mistakes" may grow up to believe these labels, even if their struggles are related to ADHD traits rather than lack of effort.

3. Social Struggles and Rejection

Many adults with ADHD experience difficulties in social interactions due to impulsivity, distractibility, or trouble reading social cues. This can lead to awkward situations, misunderstandings, or unintentional offenses, making it harder for them to maintain healthy relationships. Social rejection or feeling "different" from others can have a profound impact on self-esteem, particularly when it happens repeatedly over time.

- **Example**: A person with ADHD might interrupt others during conversations or forget important social commitments, which can lead to strained relationships. These interpersonal challenges can make them feel unworthy of strong social connections, reinforcing feelings of isolation.

4. Struggles with Emotional Regulation

ADHD is often associated with difficulties in managing emotions, which can amplify feelings of frustration, disappointment, and shame. Many adults with ADHD experience intense emotional reactions, sometimes referred to as emotional dysregulation. This heightened sensitivity, combined with frequent experiences of failure or criticism, can result in intense feelings of shame and guilt.

- **Example**: After a minor mistake, an adult with ADHD might experience overwhelming guilt or frustration, leading them to think, "I always mess things up," even if the error was trivial. This type of emotional response can further erode their self-esteem.

5. Perfectionism and Black-and-White Thinking

Some individuals with ADHD develop perfectionistic tendencies as a coping mechanism, thinking that if they could just be perfect, they wouldn't face as much criticism or failure. However, when perfectionism becomes unachievable—especially in the context of ADHD-related challenges—it often results in feelings of inadequacy. Black-and-white thinking exacerbates this, as small mistakes or imperfections may be seen as total failures.

- **Example**: An adult with ADHD might think, "If I don't get everything done perfectly at work, I'm a complete failure," setting impossible standards for themselves and reinforcing a sense of failure when those standards aren't met.

7. Difficulty with Self-Discipline and Organization

Adults with ADHD often struggle to develop consistent routines and maintain organization. While they may have the best intentions, difficulty in staying focused, managing time, and completing tasks can make even simple day-to-day responsibilities feel overwhelming. This ongoing struggle can contribute to feelings of incompetence and failure.

- **Example**: A person with ADHD may try several times to stick to an exercise routine or follow through on a personal project, only to find themselves falling behind due to procrastination or distraction. These repeated experiences of falling short can diminish their self-confidence over time.

8. Comparing Themselves to Others

People with ADHD may frequently compare themselves to their peers who appear to have their lives more together, often unaware of how hard they're working behind the scenes to manage their symptoms. This comparison can lead to feelings of inferiority and self-doubt, as they may see others accomplishing tasks that seem much more difficult for them.

- **Example**: An adult with ADHD may look at coworkers who effortlessly manage their schedules and think, "Why can't I be like them?" This constant comparison can lead them to feel that they are somehow "less capable" than others, further eroding their self-esteem.

9. Lack of Understanding or Support from Others

Many people with ADHD feel misunderstood by those around them, especially if their struggles are minimized or dismissed. Friends, family, and colleagues may fail to grasp the real impact of ADHD, assuming that the person is simply not trying hard enough. Without support or validation, individuals with ADHD may start to believe these negative messages, internalizing them as evidence of their own shortcomings.

- **Example**: If a loved one frequently says, "Why don't you just focus?" or "It's not that hard to stay organized," the person with ADHD might begin to think they are fundamentally flawed or lazy, leading to further erosion of their self-esteem.

Rebuilding Self-Esteem for Adults with ADHD

1. **Self-Awareness and Education**: Understanding ADHD and its effects can help individuals separate their self-worth from their symptoms. By recognizing that their struggles are a result of their ADHD, not personal failings, they can begin to reframe their self-perception.

2. **Focus on Strengths**: People with ADHD often possess unique strengths, such as creativity, problem-solving skills, and the ability to think outside the box. Focusing on and nurturing these strengths can help counterbalance negative self-talk.

3. **Therapy and Counseling**: Cognitive Behavioral Therapy (CBT) and other forms of counseling can be effective in helping individuals with ADHD develop healthier thought patterns, challenge negative beliefs, and rebuild their self-esteem.

4. **Mindfulness and Emotional Regulation**: Learning mindfulness techniques can help individuals with ADHD manage their emotions and reduce the intensity of their emotional reactions. Over time, this can lead to a more balanced and positive self-image.

5. **Support Systems**: Connecting with others who understand ADHD, whether through support groups or friendships, can provide validation and encouragement, helping individuals with ADHD feel less isolated in their struggles.

Low self-esteem in adults with ADHD is often a result of years of dealing with challenges that society doesn't fully understand or accommodate. By addressing these contributing factors and building healthier coping mechanisms, individuals can learn to separate their identity from their symptoms, reclaim their sense of self-worth, and lead more fulfilling lives.

PERSONAL AND INTENSE

For individuals with ADHD, self-esteem can be more fragile due to the unique challenges they face in daily life. Emotional sensitivity, negative past experiences, and difficulty managing symptoms can make them particularly vulnerable to having their self-esteem easily diminished by external forces. When someone with ADHD encounters criticism, rejection, or negativity, it can feel especially personal and intense. This vulnerability can make it easier for others—intentionally or unintentionally—to "take away" their self-esteem. Here's how and why this happens:

1. Rejection Sensitivity and Emotional Vulnerability

People with ADHD often experience **Rejection Sensitive Dysphoria (RSD)**, a condition where perceived criticism or rejection triggers an intense emotional reaction. This can make negative feedback, or perceived slights feel disproportionately hurtful. Because of RSD, a single negative comment or interaction can quickly overshadow the person's sense of self-worth.

- **Why it happens**: ADHD brains are often emotionally reactive, especially when it comes to feelings of rejection or failure. People with ADHD may internalize criticism, turning an external comment into self-criticism, making them doubt their self-worth.

- **How it happens**: A seemingly harmless remark like, "You forgot to do this again," can trigger feelings of inadequacy, leading the person with ADHD to think, "I always mess up" or "I'm not good enough." These internal dialogues snowball quickly, eroding their self-esteem.

2. **Internalized Negative Feedback Over Time**

Individuals with ADHD often receive more negative feedback than neurotypical people due to their challenges with focus, organization, and impulsivity. Over time, this consistent criticism—whether from parents, teachers, peers, or employers—can become internalized, turning into negative self-beliefs that are hard to shake. They begin to doubt their abilities, believe they are fundamentally flawed, and become more sensitive to external judgment.

- **Why it happens**: People with ADHD often grow up hearing that they need to "try harder," "focus more," or "get it together." Constant reminders of their shortcomings, especially when these struggles stem from their ADHD traits, can build up over time, leaving them feeling incapable or "different" in a negative way.

- **How it happens**: Even small critiques, such as a comment about being late or disorganized, can reinforce an individual's internal narrative of failure. Over time, these accumulated comments lead them to believe that they are not as capable as others, diminishing their self-esteem.

3. Perfectionism and Black-and-White Thinking

Many people with ADHD develop **perfectionistic tendencies** to compensate for their challenges. They might set unrealistically high standards for themselves, believing that if they achieve perfection, they can avoid criticism. However, ADHD makes it difficult to consistently meet those standards, leading to a cycle of failure and disappointment. Since individuals with ADHD often engage in **black-and-white thinking**, they may view even small mistakes as total failures, which can take a toll on their self-esteem.

- **Why it happens**: ADHD often leads to difficulties in organization, time management, and focus, making it hard to meet perfectionist goals. When they fall short, individuals with ADHD may believe they have failed completely, reinforcing a negative self-image.
- **How it happens**: When someone points out even a small flaw or oversight, it can confirm the person's internal belief that "If I'm not perfect, I'm a failure." This black-and-white thinking quickly depletes their self-esteem, as any minor mistake becomes evidence of total incompetence.

4. Lack of Validation or Support

Many people with ADHD lack understanding and validation from others. Friends, family members, or coworkers may fail to acknowledge the real challenges that come with ADHD. Instead, they might assume the person with ADHD is simply lazy, disorganized, or careless. This lack of understanding and support can make someone with ADHD feel isolated, misunderstood, and undervalued, which erodes their self-esteem.

- **Why it happens**: Without proper education about ADHD, many people assume that those with ADHD just need to try harder. This can lead to frustration for both parties, with the person with ADHD feeling like they are constantly failing despite their efforts.

- **How it happens**: When someone with ADHD struggles to meet expectations, they may hear comments like, "You're not trying hard enough" or "Why can't you just get it together?" These remarks reinforce the idea that their struggles are due to personal failings, rather than understanding ADHD as a neurological condition. This constant lack of validation can wear down their self-worth over time.

5. Comparisons to Neurotypical Standards

In a society that often measures success by neurotypical standards—like punctuality, organization, or multitasking—people with ADHD may feel that they're constantly falling short. They often compare themselves to others, seeing how effortlessly their peers manage tasks that they find difficult. When they can't meet these standards, their self-esteem suffers.

- **Why it happens**: ADHD symptoms make it harder to fit into a world designed around neurotypical behaviors. Constantly comparing themselves to others who don't face the same struggles can amplify feelings of inadequacy.

- **How it happens**: If someone with ADHD is frequently reminded of their shortcomings—whether through subtle remarks from others or their own comparisons to peers—it reinforces a sense of failure. Statements like, "Everyone else manages to do this, why can't you?" solidify their belief that they are fundamentally less capable than others.

6. Difficulty with Emotional Regulation

Many adults with ADHD struggle with **emotional dysregulation**, meaning they may have trouble controlling or processing intense emotions. When someone with ADHD encounters criticism, even if it's constructive, they may experience an emotional flood that amplifies the negativity. Their inability to regulate these emotions makes it harder to shake off hurtful comments, making them feel worse for longer periods.

- **Why it happens**: Emotional dysregulation causes them to focus intensely on negative experiences. They may fixate on hurtful comments or perceived slights, blowing them out of proportion and turning a small incident into a major blow to their self-esteem.

- **How it happens**: Even if someone casually says, "You forgot again," it can trigger an emotional response that feels overwhelming. The individual with ADHD may interpret the comment as a confirmation of their worst fears about themselves: that they are incapable or unreliable.

7. Shame and Guilt Around ADHD Symptoms

People with ADHD often experience shame related to their struggles with everyday tasks that others find simple. They may feel embarrassed about their forgetfulness, impulsivity, or inability to focus. When someone else points out these traits, it can trigger intense feelings of guilt and shame, reinforcing the belief that they are not capable of functioning "normally."

- **Why it happens**: Many people with ADHD have internalized societal expectations and often feel ashamed of their struggles. They may feel like they are "faking" their way through life, and any criticism exposes that perceived failure.

- **How it happens**: When someone makes a comment about an ADHD symptom—such as disorganization or lateness—it can cause a deep sense of shame. For example, if a coworker says, "You're always so scatterbrained," it might trigger intense feelings of worthlessness, as the individual may already be battling internal guilt over that very trait.

8. Inconsistent Performance

ADHD is often marked by inconsistency. Someone with ADHD may excel at a task one day and struggle with it the next, making it difficult to maintain confidence in their abilities. When they have a bad day or experience a failure, it can feel like confirmation of their inadequacy, and outside comments or critiques can push them further into self-doubt.

- **Why it happens**: The inconsistent nature of ADHD means that success doesn't always feel stable or reliable. A person might achieve great results one day but fail the next, leading to a constant state of self-doubt.
- **How it happens**: If someone points out an inconsistency, like, "Why were you able to do this

before but not now?" it may amplify their internal feelings of inadequacy. This reinforces the belief that they are unreliable, further damaging their self-esteem.

People with ADHD can have their self-esteem taken away easily because they often internalize external criticism, are highly sensitive to rejection, and struggle with emotional regulation. When others point out their ADHD-related struggles, even unintentionally, it can confirm their negative self-beliefs and cause intense feelings of inadequacy. Understanding these dynamics can help people with ADHD build resilience and develop healthier coping mechanisms to protect their self-esteem.

Rejection Sensitive Dysphoria (RSD) is a term that has evolved over time, primarily within the context of ADHD and broader psychological research. Here's an overview of the history and development of the concept of RSD.

Early Concepts and Theoretical Foundations

Pre-1980s: Early Observations

Before the term "Rejection Sensitive Dysphoria" was formally coined, the symptoms and experiences related to RSD were observed and described in various forms. Early psychological and psychiatric literature noted that individuals with ADHD exhibited heightened emotional responses to perceived criticism and rejection. However, these observations were often generalized and not specifically labeled as RSD.

1980s: ADHD and Emotional Sensitivity

During the 1980s, the understanding of ADHD began to evolve, with increasing recognition of the emotional and psychological challenges faced by individuals with the disorder. Researchers and clinicians noted that many people with ADHD experienced intense emotional reactions, particularly to perceived rejection or failure. This period marked the beginning of a more nuanced exploration of emotional dysregulation in ADHD.

Emergence of the Term "Rejection Sensitive Dysphoria"

1990s: Coining of the Term

The term "Rejection Sensitive Dysphoria" was introduced by Dr. William Dodson in the late 1990s. Dodson, a psychiatrist with expertise in ADHD, used the term to describe the intense emotional pain and dysphoria experienced by individuals with ADHD when they perceive rejection or criticism. This period marked a significant development in understanding the emotional aspects of ADHD, with RSD becoming a specific focus of research and clinical practice.

Early 2000s: Expanding Understanding

In the early 2000s, research and clinical observations continued to expand on the concept of RSD. The term gained traction within the ADHD community as more clinicians and researchers recognized its relevance. Studies and case reports highlighted the pervasive impact of RSD on individuals with ADHD, leading to greater awareness and acknowledgment of this emotional challenge.

Contemporary Understanding and Recognition

2010s: Increased Recognition

By the 2010s, the concept of RSD gained broader recognition within the ADHD community and beyond.

Research and clinical practice increasingly acknowledged the significant emotional impact of RSD on individuals with ADHD. However, despite growing awareness, RSD remained less well-known in mainstream medical and psychological fields.

Current Status: Ongoing Research and Awareness

Today, Rejection Sensitive Dysphoria is recognized as an important aspect of ADHD, particularly in discussions about emotional regulation and the broader implications of the disorder. Research continues to explore the neurobiological underpinnings of RSD, its relationship with other emotional and psychological conditions, and effective strategies for managing its impact. Despite this progress, RSD is still not universally recognized or fully understood within the medical community, and more research is needed to establish its diagnostic criteria and treatment approaches.

Challenges and Future Directions

Lack of Formal Recognition

One of the significant challenges facing the recognition of RSD is its absence from formal diagnostic manuals like the DSM-5. While RSD is acknowledged within the ADHD community, it is not explicitly listed as a separate diagnostic entity, leading to potential underdiagnosis and limited treatment options.

Need for Further Research

Ongoing research is crucial to further understand the neurobiological and psychological aspects of RSD, develop targeted interventions, and increase awareness within the broader medical community. Efforts to validate RSD through empirical studies and clinical trials will help establish more effective treatment protocols and improve the quality of life for individuals affected by this condition.

In summary, the history of Rejection Sensitive Dysphoria reflects a gradual evolution from early observations of emotional sensitivity in ADHD to the formal introduction and expanding recognition of RSD as a significant aspect of the disorder. Despite progress in understanding and awareness, ongoing research and advocacy are essential to fully address, and support individuals affected by RSD.

CASE STUDIES

Case Studies on the Impact of Rejection Sensitive Dysphoria (RSD)

Case Study 1: Jamie, 30

Subject: Jamie, 30 years old.

Duration of RSD Experience: Jamie has experienced RSD since childhood, exacerbated by her mother's rejection and narcissistic tendencies.

Trigger: Frequent invalidation and criticism from her mother.

Emotional Impact Over Recurring Episodes: Each episode causes Jamie intense emotional pain, leading to feelings of worthlessness and deep sadness. Over time, these episodes have increased in severity, leading to persistent anxiety and depression.

Impact on Self-Esteem: Jamie's self-esteem has been severely damaged. She internalizes her mother's rejection, believing she is inherently flawed and unworthy of love or success.

Behavior Changes: Jamie has begun to act as though she is unworthy in her day-to-day life, avoiding opportunities and interactions where she might face potential rejection. Her confidence has diminished, impacting her personal and professional relationships.

Did It Change Them? Yes, Jamie has changed significantly. Her emotional responses have become more extreme, and she has withdrawn from many areas of her life to avoid further pain.

Did They Give Up? Jamie has struggled with feelings of giving up, particularly in pursuing personal goals and maintaining relationships. The emotional burden has made it difficult for her to stay motivated.

Did They Lash Out? Jamie occasionally lashes out during intense episodes, often directed towards herself or those around her. This behavior further isolates her and strains relationships.

Outcome of Prolonged RSD: Prolonged RSD has led Jamie to experience chronic anxiety and depression. The persistent emotional pain has hindered her ability to engage in life fully and has significantly impacted her overall mental health.

Did It Break Them? The continuous emotional pain has profoundly affected Jamie's sense of self and mental health. While it has not completely broken her, it has deeply impacted her ability to live a fulfilling life.

Case Study 2: Alex, 35

Subject: Alex, 35 years old.

Duration of RSD Experience: Alex has experienced RSD for the past five years, primarily due to rejection from his spouse.

Trigger: Dismissiveness and criticism from his spouse.

Emotional Impact Over Recurring Episodes: Alex's episodes are marked by intense feelings of failure and inadequacy. The recurring nature of these episodes has led to increased anxiety and depression.

Impact on Self-Esteem: Alex's self-esteem has suffered greatly. The constant rejection has led him to question his value and abilities in the relationship.

Behavior Changes: Alex has begun to act in ways that reflect his feelings of worthlessness, withdrawing from social interactions and avoiding situations where he might face further rejection.

Did It Change Them? Yes, Alex's emotional responses have become more volatile, and his confidence in relationships has diminished.

Did They Give Up? Alex has struggled with feelings of giving up on improving his relationship and personal aspirations, feeling that any effort is futile.

Did They Lash Out? Alex has lashed out during episodes, often directing his frustration and hurt towards his spouse, leading to further relationship strain.

Outcome of Prolonged RSD: Prolonged RSD has resulted in chronic relationship issues and deepened feelings of inadequacy. Alex's ongoing emotional distress has negatively impacted his overall well-being and life satisfaction.

Did It Break Them? The persistent emotional pain has significantly impacted Alex's mental health, but he is still working towards managing his RSD and improving his situation.

Case Study 3: Taylor, 28

Subject: Taylor, 28 years old.

Duration of RSD Experience: Taylor has dealt with RSD for approximately three years, triggered by repeated career rejections.

Trigger: Job application rejections and negative feedback from interviews.

Emotional Impact Over Recurring Episodes: Each rejection exacerbates Taylor's feelings of failure and hopelessness. The recurring nature of these episodes has led to chronic stress and anxiety.

Impact on Self-Esteem: Taylor's self-esteem has been severely impacted. He feels as though his career aspirations are unattainable, leading to a diminished sense of self-worth.

Behavior Changes: Taylor has started to avoid applying for new jobs and has become less proactive in seeking career advancement. His fear of rejection has paralyzed him.

Did It Change Them: Taylor's approach to career and personal development has changed. He now avoids taking risks and has become more passive in his professional life.

Did They Give Up? Taylor has come close to giving up on his career goals, feeling overwhelmed by the continuous rejections and emotional burden.

Did They Lash Out? Taylor has not lashed out at others but has directed his frustration inward, leading to self-criticism and negative self-talk.

Outcome of Prolonged RSD: Prolonged RSD has resulted in career stagnation and persistent mental health issues. Taylor's long-term emotional pain has hindered his professional growth and overall life satisfaction.

Did It Break Them? The emotional strain has profoundly impacted Taylor's motivation and self-esteem. While it has not completely broken him, it has significantly affected his ability to pursue his goals.

Case Study 4: Jordan, 24

Subject: Jordan, 24 years old.

Duration of RSD Experience: Jordan has experienced RSD for about two years, primarily related to peer rejection and social interactions.

Trigger: Exclusion from social activities and perceived slights by peers.

Emotional Impact Over Recurring Episodes: Jordan feels deeply hurt and isolated after each episode. The recurring rejections have led to increased social anxiety and depression.

Impact on Self-Esteem: Jordan's self-esteem has suffered as he internalizes the rejection. He feels unworthy of social connections and validation.

Behavior Changes: Jordan has become increasingly withdrawn and avoids social situations to prevent further rejection. His social life has diminished significantly.

Did It Change Them? Yes, Jordan has changed in terms of his social behavior. His fear of rejection has led him to isolate himself from others.

Did They Give Up? Jordan has struggled with feelings of giving up on social interactions and friendships, feeling that they are not worth the emotional pain.

Did They Lash Out? Jordan has not lashed out at others but has become more self-critical, which exacerbates his feelings of isolation.

Outcome of Prolonged RSD: Prolonged RSD has led to severe social withdrawal and decreased self-esteem.

Jordan's long-term emotional distress has significantly impacted his quality of life.

Did It Break Them? The ongoing emotional pain has deeply affected Jordan's social well-being and self-esteem, making it difficult for him to engage in fulfilling social interactions.

Case Study 5: Morgan, 32

Subject: Morgan, 32 years old.

Duration of RSD Experience: Morgan has been experiencing RSD for over four years, primarily related to workplace performance evaluations.

Trigger: Negative feedback and criticism from supervisors.

Emotional Impact Over Recurring Episodes: Morgan experiences profound feelings of inadequacy and failure after each episode. The emotional distress from performance-related feedback is significant.

Impact on Self-Esteem: Morgan's self-esteem has been deeply affected by the recurring criticism. She feels incapable and unworthy of professional success.

Behavior Changes: Morgan has become hesitant to take on new responsibilities and avoid opportunities for advancement due to fear of further rejection.

Did It Change Them? Yes, Morgan's professional confidence has diminished. Her approach to work has become more cautious and less ambitious.

Did They Give Up? Morgan has not entirely given up but has become less proactive in pursuing career goals. The fear of rejection has hindered her progress.

Did They Lash Out? Morgan has not lashed out at others but has engaged in negative self-talk and self-criticism, affecting her self-esteem.

Outcome of Prolonged RSD: Prolonged RSD has led to career stagnation and persistent anxiety. Morgan's ongoing emotional pain has impeded her professional development and overall job satisfaction.

Did It Break Them? The emotional strain has significantly impacted Morgan's professional life and self-esteem, although it has not completely broken her spirit.

Case Study 6: Riley, 26

Subject: Riley, 26 years old.

Duration of RSD Experience: Riley has experienced RSD for the past three years, primarily related to academic rejections.

Trigger: Rejections from academic programs and scholarship applications.

Emotional Impact Over Recurring Episodes: Riley feels intense disappointment and self-doubt after each rejection. The emotional impact is deep, affecting her motivation and self-worth.

Impact on Self-Esteem: Riley's self-esteem has been negatively affected by the repeated academic failures. She feels incapable of achieving her educational goals.

Behavior Changes: Riley has become discouraged and less motivated to pursue further academic opportunities. She avoids applying for new programs due to fear of rejection.

Did It Change Them? Yes, Riley's academic aspirations have been significantly impacted. Her confidence in her abilities has diminished, affecting her overall motivation.

Did They Give Up? Riley has struggled with feelings of giving up on her academic dreams, feeling that further attempts will only lead to more rejection.

Did They Lash Out? Riley has not lashed out at others but has engaged in self-criticism and negative self-talk, exacerbating her feelings of inadequacy.

Outcome of Prolonged RSD: Prolonged RSD has led to a decreased sense of self-worth and academic disengagement. Riley's long-term emotional pain has hindered her educational progress and personal development.

Did It Break Them? The continuous emotional distress has significantly impacted Riley's academic motivation and self-esteem, although it has not completely broken her.

Case Study 7: Casey, 40

Subject: Casey, 40 years old.

Duration of RSD Experience: Casey has been experiencing RSD for over six years, triggered by marital issues and partner rejection.

Trigger: Frequent arguments and emotional distance from her spouse.

Emotional Impact Over Recurring Episodes: Each episode exacerbates Casey's feelings of inadequacy and emotional pain. The recurring nature of these episodes has led to chronic anxiety and depression.

Impact on Self-Esteem: Casey's self-esteem has been severely damaged by the perceived rejection from her spouse. She feels unworthy of love and support.

Behavior Changes: Casey has become more withdrawn in her marriage, avoiding discussions and interactions with her spouse. Her self-worth is deeply affected.

Did It Change Them? Yes, Casey's emotional responses and behavior towards her spouse have changed. She is more cautious and less engaged in the relationship.

Did They Give Up? Casey has struggled with feelings of giving up on her marriage, feeling that her efforts are futile.

Did They Lash Out? Casey has lashed out at her spouse during intense episodes, leading to increased marital conflict and emotional distance.

Outcome of Prolonged RSD: Prolonged RSD has led to significant marital problems and persistent emotional distress. Casey's long-term struggle has deeply affected her relationship and mental health.

Did It Break Them? The ongoing emotional pain has profoundly impacted Casey's relationship and self-esteem, making it difficult for her to maintain a fulfilling marriage.

Case Study 8: Drew, 29

Subject: Drew, 29 years old.

Duration of RSD Experience: Drew has experienced RSD for about five years, triggered by persistent failures in job applications and career setbacks.

Trigger: Continuous rejections from job applications and failed promotions.

Emotional Impact Over Recurring Episodes: Drew experiences deep feelings of failure and hopelessness after each setback. The recurring rejections have led to heightened anxiety and depression.

Impact on Self-Esteem: Drew's self-esteem has been significantly impacted by the ongoing career failures. He feels incapable of achieving professional success.

Behavior Changes: Drew has become hesitant to pursue new job opportunities and has withdrawn from professional networking. His confidence in his career has diminished.

Did It Change Them? Yes, Drew's professional confidence and motivation have decreased. He is less proactive in seeking career advancement.

Did They Give Up? Drew has struggled with feelings of giving up on his career ambitions, feeling that further efforts will only lead to more rejection.

Did They Lash Out? Drew has not lashed out at others but has engaged in negative self-talk and self-criticism, affecting his overall mental health.

Outcome of Prolonged RSD: Prolonged RSD has led to career stagnation and chronic anxiety. Drew's long-term emotional distress has impacted his professional development and overall life satisfaction.

Did It Break Them? The ongoing emotional pain has significantly affected Drew's career and self-esteem, although it has not completely broken his spirit.

Case Study 9: Sam, 38

Subject: Sam, 38 years old.

Duration of RSD Experience: Sam has experienced RSD for the past seven years, triggered by repeated rejection from social circles and friendships.

Trigger: Exclusion from social activities and perceived neglect by friends.

Emotional Impact Over Recurring Episodes: Sam experiences intense feelings of loneliness and rejection. The emotional impact is profound, affecting his social interactions and overall mood.

Impact on Self-Esteem: Sam's self-esteem has been deeply affected by the ongoing rejection. He feels unworthy of meaningful friendships and social connections.

Behavior Changes: Sam has become increasingly isolated and avoids social interactions to prevent further rejection. His social life has been significantly impacted.

Did It Change Them? Yes, Sam's social behavior and confidence have been affected. He is more withdrawn and less engaged in social activities.

Did They Give Up? Sam has struggled with feelings of giving up on forming new friendships and maintaining existing relationships.

Did They Lash Out? Sam has not lashed out at others but has become more self-critical, which exacerbates his feelings of isolation.

Outcome of Prolonged RSD: Prolonged RSD has led to severe social withdrawal and decreased self-esteem. Sam's long-term emotional distress has significantly impacted his quality of life.

Did It Break Them? The continuous emotional pain has deeply affected Sam's social well-being and self-esteem, although it has not completely broken him.

Case Study 10: Pat, 45

Subject: Pat, 45 years old.

Duration of RSD Experience: Pat has experienced RSD for over eight years, primarily triggered by frequent failures and rejections in personal goals and aspirations.

Trigger: Repeated failures in personal projects and pursuits.

Emotional Impact Over Recurring Episodes: Pat feels profound disappointment and self-doubt after each failure. The recurring nature of these experiences has led to persistent emotional pain and frustration.

Impact on Self-Esteem: Pat's self-esteem has been deeply impacted by the repeated failures. He feels incapable of achieving his personal goals and has internalized the rejection.

Behavior Changes: Pat has become less ambitious and more cautious, avoiding new projects or goals due to fear of further failure and rejection.

Did It Change Them? Yes, Pat's approach to personal goals and ambitions has changed. He is less proactive and more hesitant to take risks.

Did They Give Up? Pat has struggled with feelings of giving up on personal aspirations, feeling that continued efforts will only result in more rejection.

Did They Lash Out? Pat has not lashed out at others but has engaged in intense self-criticism, leading to a decreased sense of self-worth.

Outcome of Prolonged RSD: Prolonged RSD has led to diminished personal goals and chronic emotional distress. Pat's long-term struggle has impacted his overall motivation and well-being.

Did It Break Them? The ongoing emotional pain has significantly affected Pat's ability to pursue personal aspirations and maintain a positive self-image, although it has not completely broken him.

These case studies illustrate the diverse experiences and impacts of RSD on individuals. Each person's journey with RSD is unique, but the common thread is the profound emotional pain and psychological effects stemming from perceived rejection.

Case Studies on the Impact of Rejection Sensitive Dysphoria (RSD)

Case Study 1: Jamie, 30

Subject: Jamie, 30 years old.

Duration of RSD Experience: Jamie has experienced RSD since childhood, exacerbated by her mother's rejection and narcissistic tendencies.

Trigger: Frequent invalidation and criticism from her mother.

Emotional Impact Over Recurring Episodes: Each episode causes Jamie intense emotional pain, leading to feelings of worthlessness and deep sadness. Over time, these episodes have increased in severity, leading to persistent anxiety and depression.

Impact on Self-Esteem: Jamie's self-esteem has been severely damaged. She internalizes her mother's rejection, believing she is inherently flawed and unworthy of love or success.

Behavior Changes: Jamie has begun to act as though she is unworthy in her day-to-day life, avoiding opportunities and interactions where she might face potential rejection. Her confidence has diminished, impacting her personal and professional relationships.

Did It Change Them: Yes, Jamie has changed significantly. Her emotional responses have become more extreme, and she has withdrawn from many areas of her life to avoid further pain.

Did They Give Up: Jamie has struggled with feelings of giving up, particularly in pursuing personal goals and maintaining relationships. The emotional burden has made it difficult for her to stay motivated.

Did They Lash Out: Jamie occasionally lashes out during intense episodes, often directed towards herself or those around her. This behavior further isolates her and strains relationships.

Outcome of Prolonged RSD: Prolonged RSD has led Jamie to experience chronic anxiety and depression. The persistent emotional pain has hindered her ability to engage in life fully and has significantly impacted her overall mental health.

Did It Break Them: The continuous emotional pain has profoundly affected Jamie's sense of self and mental health. While it has not completely broken her, it has deeply impacted her ability to live a fulfilling life.

Case Study 2: Alex, 35

Subject: Alex, 35 years old.

Duration of RSD Experience: Alex has experienced RSD for the past five years, primarily due to rejection from his spouse.

Trigger: Dismissiveness and criticism from his spouse.

Emotional Impact Over Recurring Episodes: Alex's episodes are marked by intense feelings of failure and inadequacy. The recurring nature of these episodes has led to increased anxiety and depression.

Impact on Self-Esteem: Alex's self-esteem has suffered greatly. The constant rejection has led him to question his value and abilities in the relationship.

Behavior Changes: Alex has begun to act in ways that reflect his feelings of worthlessness, withdrawing from social interactions and avoiding situations where he might face further rejection.

Did It Change Them: Yes, Alex's emotional responses have become more volatile, and his confidence in relationships has diminished.

Did They Give Up: Alex has struggled with feelings of giving up on improving his relationship and personal aspirations, feeling that any effort is futile.

Did They Lash Out: Alex has lashed out during episodes, often directing his frustration and hurt towards his spouse, leading to further relationship strain.

Outcome of Prolonged RSD: Prolonged RSD has resulted in chronic relationship issues and deepened feelings of inadequacy. Alex's ongoing emotional distress has negatively impacted his overall well-being and life satisfaction.

Did It Break Them: The persistent emotional pain has significantly impacted Alex's mental health, but he is still working towards managing his RSD and improving his situation.

Case Study 3: Taylor, 28

Subject: Taylor, 28 years old.

Duration of RSD Experience: Taylor has dealt with RSD for approximately three years, triggered by repeated career rejections.

Trigger: Job application rejections and negative feedback from interviews.

Emotional Impact Over Recurring Episodes: Each rejection exacerbates Taylor's feelings of failure and hopelessness. The recurring nature of these episodes has led to chronic stress and anxiety.

Impact on Self-Esteem: Taylor's self-esteem has been severely impacted. He feels as though his career aspirations are unattainable, leading to a diminished sense of self-worth.

Behavior Changes: Taylor has started to avoid applying for new jobs and has become less proactive in seeking career advancement due to fear of rejection.

Did It Change Them: Yes, Taylor's approach to career and personal development has changed. He now avoids taking risks and has become more passive in his professional life.

Did They Give Up: Taylor has come close to giving up on his career goals, feeling overwhelmed by the continuous rejections and emotional burden.

Did They Lash Out: Taylor has not lashed out at others but has directed his frustration inward, leading to self-criticism and negative self-talk.

Outcome of Prolonged RSD: Prolonged RSD has resulted in career stagnation and persistent mental health issues. Taylor's long-term emotional pain has hindered his professional growth and overall life satisfaction.

Did It Break Them: The emotional strain has profoundly impacted Taylor's motivation and self-esteem. While it has not completely broken him, it has significantly affected his ability to pursue his goals.

Case Study 4: Jordan, 24

Subject: Jordan, 24 years old.

Duration of RSD Experience: Jordan has experienced RSD for about two years, primarily related to peer rejection and social interactions.

Trigger: Exclusion from social activities and perceived slights by peers.

Emotional Impact Over Recurring Episodes: Jordan feels deeply hurt and isolated after each episode. The recurring rejections have led to increased social anxiety and depression.

Impact on Self-Esteem: Jordan's self-esteem has suffered as he internalizes the rejection. He feels unworthy of social connections and validation.

Behavior Changes: Jordan has become increasingly withdrawn and avoids social situations to prevent further rejection. His social life has diminished significantly.

Did It Change Them: Yes, Jordan has changed in terms of his social behavior. His fear of rejection has led him to isolate himself from others.

Did They Give Up: Jordan has struggled with feelings of giving up on social interactions and friendships, feeling that they are not worth the emotional pain.

Did They Lash Out: Jordan has not lashed out at others but has become more self-critical, which exacerbates his feelings of isolation.

Outcome of Prolonged RSD: Prolonged RSD has led to severe social withdrawal and decreased self-esteem. Jordan's long-term emotional distress has significantly impacted his quality of life.

Did It Break Them: The ongoing emotional pain has deeply affected Jordan's social well-being and self-esteem, making it difficult for him to engage in fulfilling social interactions.

Case Study 5: Morgan, 32

Subject: Morgan, 32 years old.

Duration of RSD Experience: Morgan has been experiencing RSD for over four years, primarily related to workplace performance evaluations.

Trigger: Negative feedback and criticism from supervisors.

Emotional Impact Over Recurring Episodes: Morgan experiences profound feelings of inadequacy and failure after each episode. The emotional distress from performance-related feedback is significant.

Impact on Self-Esteem: Morgan's self-esteem has been deeply affected by the recurring criticism. She feels incapable and unworthy of professional success.

Behavior Changes: Morgan has become hesitant to take on new responsibilities and avoid opportunities for advancement due to fear of further rejection.

Did It Change Them: Yes, Morgan's professional confidence has diminished. Her approach to work has become more cautious and less ambitious.

Did They Give Up: Morgan has not entirely given up but has become less proactive in pursuing career goals. The fear of rejection has hindered her progress.

Did They Lash Out: Morgan has not lashed out at others but has engaged in negative self-talk and self-criticism, affecting her self-esteem.

Outcome of Prolonged RSD: Prolonged RSD has led to career stagnation and persistent anxiety. Morgan's ongoing emotional pain has impeded her professional development and overall job satisfaction.

Did It Break Them: The emotional strain has significantly impacted Morgan's professional life and self-esteem, although it has not completely broken her spirit.

Case Study 6: Riley, 26

Subject: Riley, 26 years old.

Duration of RSD Experience: Riley has experienced RSD for the past three years, primarily related to academic rejections.

Trigger: Rejections from academic programs and scholarship applications.

Emotional Impact Over Recurring Episodes: Riley feels intense disappointment and self-doubt after each rejection. The emotional impact is deep, affecting her motivation and self-worth.

Impact on Self-Esteem: Riley's self-esteem has been negatively affected by the repeated academic failures. She feels incapable of achieving her educational goals.

Behavior Changes: Riley has become discouraged and less motivated to pursue further academic opportunities.

She avoids applying for new programs due to fear of rejection.

Did It Change Them: Yes, Riley's academic aspirations have been significantly impacted. Her confidence in her abilities has diminished, affecting her overall motivation.

Did They Give Up: Riley has struggled with feelings of giving up on her academic dreams, feeling that further attempts will only lead to more rejection.

Did They Lash Out: Riley has not lashed out at others but has engaged in self-criticism and negative self-talk, exacerbating her feelings of inadequacy.

Outcome of Prolonged RSD: Prolonged RSD has led to a decreased sense of self-worth and academic disengagement. Riley's long-term emotional pain has hindered her educational progress and personal development.

Did It Break Them: The continuous emotional distress has significantly impacted Riley's academic motivation and self-esteem, although it has not completely broken her.

Case Study 7: Casey, 40

Subject: Casey, 40 years old.

Duration of RSD Experience: Casey has been experiencing RSD for over six years, triggered by marital issues and partner rejection.

Trigger: Frequent arguments and emotional distance from her spouse.

Emotional Impact Over Recurring Episodes: Each episode exacerbates Casey's feelings of inadequacy and emotional pain. The recurring nature of these episodes has led to chronic anxiety and depression.

Impact on Self-Esteem: Casey's self-esteem has been severely damaged by the perceived rejection from her spouse. She feels unworthy of love and support.

Behavior Changes: Casey has become more withdrawn in her marriage, avoiding discussions and interactions with her spouse. Her self-worth is deeply affected.

Did It Change Them: Yes, Casey's emotional responses and behavior towards her spouse have changed. She is more cautious and less engaged in the relationship.

Did They Give Up: Casey has struggled with feelings of giving up on her marriage, feeling that her efforts are futile.

Did They Lash Out: Casey has lashed out at her spouse during intense episodes, leading to increased marital conflict and emotional distance.

Outcome of Prolonged RSD: Prolonged RSD has led to significant marital problems and persistent emotional distress. Casey's long-term struggle has deeply affected her relationship and mental health.

Did It Break Them: The ongoing emotional pain has profoundly impacted Casey's relationship and self-esteem, making it difficult for her to maintain a fulfilling marriage.

Case Study 8: Drew, 29

Subject: Drew, 29 years old.

Duration of RSD Experience: Drew has experienced RSD for about five years, triggered by persistent failures in job applications and career setbacks.

Trigger: Continuous rejections from job applications and failed promotions.

Emotional Impact Over Recurring Episodes: Drew experiences deep feelings of failure and hopelessness after each setback. The recurring rejections have led to heightened anxiety and depression.

Impact on Self-Esteem: Drew's self-esteem has been significantly impacted by the ongoing career failures. He feels incapable of achieving professional success.

Behavior Changes: Drew has become hesitant to pursue new job opportunities and has withdrawn from professional networking. His confidence in his career has diminished.

Did It Change Them: Yes, Drew's professional confidence and motivation have decreased. He is less proactive in seeking career advancement.

Did They Give Up: Drew has struggled with feelings of giving up on his career ambitions, feeling that further efforts will only lead to more rejection.

Did They Lash Out: Drew has not lashed out at others but has engaged in negative self-talk and self-criticism, affecting his overall mental health.

Outcome of Prolonged RSD: Prolonged RSD has led to career stagnation and chronic anxiety. Drew's long-term emotional distress has impacted his professional development and overall life satisfaction.

Did It Break Them: The ongoing emotional pain has significantly affected Drew's career and self-esteem, although it has not completely broken his spirit.

Case Study 9: Sam, 38

Subject: Sam, 38 years old.

Duration of RSD Experience: Sam has experienced RSD for the past seven years, triggered by repeated rejection from social circles and friendships.

Trigger: Exclusion from social activities and perceived neglect by friends.

Emotional Impact Over Recurring Episodes: Sam experiences intense feelings of loneliness and rejection. The emotional impact is profound, affecting his social interactions and overall mood.

Impact on Self-Esteem: Sam's self-esteem has been deeply affected by the ongoing rejection. He feels unworthy of meaningful friendships and social connections.

Behavior Changes: Sam has become increasingly isolated and avoids social interactions to prevent further rejection. His social life has been significantly impacted.

Did It Change Them: Yes, Sam's social behavior and confidence have been affected. He is more withdrawn and less engaged in social activities.

Did They Give Up: Sam has struggled with feelings of giving up on forming new friendships and maintaining existing relationships.

Did They Lash Out: Sam has not lashed out at others but has become more self-critical, which exacerbates his feelings of isolation.

Outcome of Prolonged RSD: Prolonged RSD has led to severe social withdrawal and decreased self-esteem. Sam's long-term emotional distress has significantly impacted his quality of life.

Did It Break Them: The continuous emotional pain has deeply affected Sam's social well-being and self-esteem, although it has not completely broken him.

Case Study 10: Pat, 45

Subject: Pat, 45 years old.

Duration of RSD Experience: Pat has experienced RSD for over eight years, primarily triggered by frequent failures and rejections in personal goals and aspirations.

Trigger: Repeated failures in personal projects and pursuits.

Emotional Impact Over Recurring Episodes: Pat feels profound disappointment and self-doubt after each failure. The recurring nature of these experiences has led to persistent emotional pain and frustration.

Impact on Self-Esteem: Pat's self-esteem has been deeply impacted by the repeated failures. He feels incapable of achieving his personal goals and has internalized the rejection.

Behavior Changes: Pat has become less ambitious and more cautious, avoiding new projects or goals due to fear of further failure and rejection.

Did It Change Them: Yes, Pat's approach to personal goals and ambitions has changed. He is less proactive and more hesitant to take risks.

Did They Give Up: Pat has struggled with feelings of giving up on personal aspirations, feeling that continued efforts will only result in more rejection.

Did They Lash Out: Pat has not lashed out at others but has engaged in intense self-criticism, leading to a decreased sense of self-worth.

Outcome of Prolonged RSD: Prolonged RSD has led to diminished personal goals and chronic emotional distress. Pat's long-term struggle has impacted his overall motivation and well-being.

Did It Break Them: The ongoing emotional pain has significantly affected Pat's ability to pursue personal aspirations and maintain a positive self-image, although it has not completely broken him.

These case studies illustrate the diverse experiences and impacts of RSD on individuals. Each person's journey with RSD is unique, but the common thread is the profound emotional pain and

TOXIC ENVIRONMENT

This is what happens when ADHD RSD has been pushed to their limit.

Lashing out

When someone with ADHD and Rejection Sensitive Dysphoria (RSD) is exposed to repetitive insults, blame, or projection of faults onto them, their emotional responses can be intensely heightened due to the nature of RSD. Here's a detailed explanation of why they might lash out physically in such situations:

Emotional Sensitivity and RSD

1. **Intense Emotional Reaction**: Individuals with RSD experience an exaggerated emotional response to perceived rejection or criticism. This heightened sensitivity makes them more vulnerable to emotional pain. When insults and blame are repeated, the emotional distress compounds, leading to an overwhelming sense of hurt and frustration.

2. **Emotional Overload**: Continuous negative feedback can lead to emotional overload. For someone with RSD, the emotional pain from repeated rejection or criticism is not just a passing feeling but a deeply felt wound that triggers significant stress and anxiety. This state of emotional overload can impair their ability to think clearly and manage their reactions effectively.

3. **Inability to Self-Regulate**: RSD affects emotional regulation, making it difficult for individuals to manage their feelings in the face of continuous negative stimuli. The frustration and hurt from repeated insults can escalate quickly, overwhelming their coping mechanisms and potentially leading to physical outbursts as a form of release.

Psychological Mechanisms

1. **Defensive Response**: When someone with RSD perceives that they are being unfairly attacked or blamed, their defensive mechanisms may be triggered. This defense can manifest as a physical reaction, especially if they feel cornered or helpless. The lashing out is an attempt to protect themselves from further emotional harm.

2. **Projection of Internal Conflict**: People with RSD might internalize the blame and criticism they receive, leading to heightened self-criticism and self-doubt. This internal conflict can create a sense of injustice or rage, which might be projected outward physically if they feel that verbal or emotional avenues for expressing their distress are ineffective or unsafe.

3. **Lack of Constructive Outlets**: If individuals with RSD do not have access to healthy coping strategies or supportive environments, they might resort to physical reactions as a way to express their intense emotions. The lack of constructive outlets for their pain can result in them lashing out as an immediate but unproductive form of emotional release.

Social and Environmental Factors

1. **Power Dynamics and Perceived Control**: Repeated insults and blame can create a power imbalance, making the individual feel powerless and oppressed. In such situations, a physical response can be an attempt to regain a sense of control or assertiveness in an environment where they feel dominated or disempowered.

2. **Escalation of Conflict**: Continuous negative interactions can escalate conflicts. When verbal and emotional exchanges fail to address the pain or resolve the conflict, physical reactions may emerge as a heightened response to ongoing aggression or hostility.

3. **Lack of Empathy from Others**: If the person causing the pain lacks empathy or understanding, it exacerbates the emotional distress for the individual with RSD. The perceived lack of compassion or acknowledgment can lead to frustration, which might manifest as physical aggression if the individual feels that their emotional pain is being dismissed or invalidated.

Bad Environment

The physical lashing out in response to repeated insults, blame, or projections of faults is often a manifestation of the deep emotional pain and frustration experienced by someone with ADHD and RSD. Their heightened sensitivity, emotional overload, impaired self-regulation, and defensive responses contribute to this reaction. Addressing these issues involves understanding their emotional landscape, providing supportive and empathetic interactions, and fostering healthy coping mechanisms to manage intense emotional responses effectively.

Here is a list of behaviors and actions that can trigger someone with ADHD and Rejection Sensitive Dysphoria (RSD) to lash out:

1. **Not Allowing a Break**: Forcing someone to remain in a high-conflict situation without allowing them to step away and gain composure.
2. **Constant Criticism**: Repeatedly providing negative feedback without offering any positive reinforcement or constructive suggestions.
3. **Verbal Beratement**: Forcing someone to endure a prolonged session of verbal insults or attacks.
4. **Dismissal of Feelings**: Ignoring or invalidating their emotional responses and dismissing their concerns as unimportant.
5. **Unfair Blame**: Placing undue blame on them for issues or problems, especially if they are not responsible.
6. **Public Embarrassment**: Criticizing or belittling them in front of others, which can amplify feelings of shame and rejection.

7. **Personal Insults**: Targeting personal traits or behaviors for ridicule or derogatory comments.

8. **Intense Confrontations**: Engaging in heated arguments without allowing time for calm discussion or resolution.

9. **Overwhelming Negative Feedback**: Providing a barrage of negative comments or criticisms all at once, without any positive balance.

10. **Manipulating or Controlling**: Using emotional manipulation or controlling behaviors to assert dominance or control over them.

11. **Ignoring Boundaries**: Disregarding their personal boundaries and continuing to engage in behavior that they find distressing or invasive.

12. **Gaslighting**: Making them doubt their own perceptions or reality, leading to increased emotional confusion and distress.

13. **Repeated Rejection**: Continuously rejecting or dismissing their attempts to connect, contribute, or participate.

14. **Belittling Achievements**: Minimizing or mocking their accomplishments and successes, undermining their self-worth.

15. **Inconsistent Expectations**: Having unpredictable or inconsistent standards and expectations, leading to confusion and frustration.

16. **Withholding Support**: Denying emotional or practical support during times of need, adding to their sense of isolation.

17. **Unfair Comparisons**: Comparing them unfavorably to others, which can exacerbate feelings of inadequacy and self-doubt.

18. **Threatening Consequences**: Using threats of punishment or negative consequences as a form of control or coercion.

19. **Verbal Aggression**: Using aggressive or hostile language that escalates the emotional intensity of the interaction.

20. **Invalidating Responses**: Offering dismissive or invalidating responses to their expressions of distress or frustration.

21. **Expecting Immediate Compliance**: Demanding immediate compliance or agreement without allowing time for thoughtful consideration or response.

22. **Ignoring Needs**: Failing to acknowledge or address their emotional or psychological needs during interactions.

23. **Shaming**: Using shame as a tactic to control or influence their behavior, which can deepen feelings of rejection.

24. **Micro-Management**: Excessively controlling or scrutinizing their actions, leading to frustration and a sense of being stifled.

25. **Overloading with Tasks**: Assigning an excessive number of tasks or responsibilities without adequate support or resources.

26. **Disrespecting Personal Space**: Violating their personal space or boundaries, which can feel threatening and provoke defensive reactions.

27. **Engaging in Power Struggles**: Participating in power struggles or arguments that escalate conflicts rather than resolving them.

28. **Contradicting Statements**: Offering contradictory or confusing statements that increase emotional distress and frustration.

29. **Ignoring Achievements**: Failing to acknowledge or celebrate their successes, which can diminish their self-esteem.

30. **Overly Critical Feedback**: Providing feedback that is overly harsh or focused solely on faults without any constructive elements.

31. **Making Unfair Comparisons**: Comparing them unfavorably to others, which can amplify feelings of inadequacy.

32. **Dismissing Efforts**: Belittling or ignoring their efforts or attempts to improve or resolve situations.

33. **Undermining Confidence**: Engaging in behaviors that undermine their confidence or self-esteem, leading to increased self-doubt.

34. **Micromanaging**: Excessively controlling or nitpicking their actions and decisions, causing frustration and feelings of incompetence.

35. **Frequent Interruptions**: Interrupting or talking over them, preventing them from expressing their thoughts and feelings fully.

36. **Ignoring Emotional Reactions**: Failing to acknowledge or address their emotional reactions, leading to feelings of invalidation.

37. **Using Ultimatums**: Applying ultimatums or making demands that leave no room for negotiation or compromise.

38. **Belittling Contributions**: Minimizing or dismissing their contributions or input, which can lead to feelings of worthlessness.

39. **Using Sarcasm**: Employing sarcasm or mocking tones that can be hurtful and dismissive of their feelings.

40. **Public Criticism**: Criticizing or reprimanding them in front of others, which can intensify feelings of embarrassment and rejection.

41. **Ignoring Feedback**: Disregarding their feedback or input, leading to a sense of being undervalued or unimportant.

42. **Using Guilt**: Employing guilt-tripping tactics to influence their behavior or decisions, which can be emotionally distressing.

43. **Withholding Affection**: Withholding positive reinforcement or affection during conflicts, exacerbating feelings of rejection.

44. **Overloading with Information**: Providing excessive or contradictory information that leads to confusion and frustration.

45. **Invalidating Feelings**: Telling them that their feelings are irrational or unwarranted, leading to further emotional distress.

46. **Challenging Integrity**: Questioning their character or integrity in a way that feels personal and attacking.

47. **Publicly Exposing Mistakes**: Highlighting or exposing their mistakes or failures publicly, increasing feelings of shame.

48. **Demanding Perfection**: Expecting unrealistic standards of perfection without acknowledging their efforts or progress.

49. **Failing to Acknowledge Efforts**: Not recognizing or appreciating their efforts, which can lead to feelings of invisibility and inadequacy.

50. **Reinforcing Negative Self-Perceptions**: Acting in ways that reinforce their negative self-perceptions or self-doubt, leading to emotional distress.

These behaviors can contribute to the emotional turmoil experienced by individuals with ADHD and RSD, potentially leading to intense reactions and feelings of frustration. Understanding these triggers can help in developing more empathetic and supportive interactions

Example

woman with ADHD and Rejection Sensitive Dysphoria (RSD) is experiencing a deeply challenging and distressing emotional state due to her interactions with her partner, who displays narcissistic traits. Here's an in-depth look at what she is going through:

Emotional and Psychological Impact

1. **Overwhelming Fear and Anxiety**: The constant exposure to anger, insults, and belittlement triggers intense fear and anxiety. Her partner's unpredictable and aggressive behavior makes her feel constantly on edge, unsure of when the next emotional attack might come. This heightened state of alertness contributes to chronic stress and anxiety.

2. **Emotional Shutdown**: When faced with continuous beratement or narcissistic rage, she may shut down emotionally as a protective mechanism. This shutdown is a response to feeling overwhelmed and powerless, leading her to become silent or unable to articulate her feelings or defend herself effectively.

3. **Increased Sensitivity to Rejection**: Due to her RSD, even minor criticisms or perceived rejections can feel intensely painful. Her partner's constant negative feedback and insults exacerbate this sensitivity,

making every interaction feel like a personal attack. This magnifies her emotional suffering and reinforces her feelings of inadequacy.

4. **Self-Blame and Guilt**: The partner's manipulative behavior, including turning her words against her and making her feel at fault, can lead her to internalize the blame. She may start to question her own worth and believe that she is at fault for the conflicts or her partner's behavior. This self-blame is compounded by the partner's lack of remorse or empathy.

5. **Post-Traumatic Stress Symptoms**: The continuous exposure to narcissistic rage and emotional abuse can result in symptoms similar to PTSD. This may include flashbacks, heightened startle responses, and intrusive thoughts. The woman might experience a pervasive sense of fear and helplessness that affects her ability to function normally in daily life.

6. **Feelings of Worthlessness**: The repeated insults and the partner's refusal to acknowledge her feelings can lead her to feel worthless. She may internalize the negative messages she receives, believing that she is fundamentally flawed or undeserving of respect and love.

7. **Frozen Response to Conflict**: The emotional and psychological trauma from these interactions can cause her to freeze in situations where she feels attacked or criticized. This freeze response is a result of the overwhelming fear and past trauma, making it difficult for her to respond or protect herself during conflicts.

8. **Emotional Isolation**: The intense emotional pain and fear associated with her partner's behavior may lead her to withdraw from social interactions and isolate herself. She may feel disconnected from others and hesitant to seek support, further exacerbating her feelings of loneliness and despair.

9. **Difficulty in Trusting Others**: The ongoing emotional abuse can erode her ability to trust others. She might start to generalize her partner's behavior to others, assuming that they too will be untrustworthy or harmful, which can affect her relationships outside of the marriage.

10. **Long-Term Psychological Damage**: Prolonged exposure to this type of emotional abuse can have long-term psychological effects, including chronic depression, severe anxiety, and deep-seated trauma.

The woman may struggle with self-esteem issues and find it challenging to recover her sense of self-worth and confidence.

Coping and Support

To address these challenges, it's crucial for her to seek professional support, such as therapy or counseling, to help her process the trauma, rebuild self-esteem, and develop effective coping strategies. Support from friends or family who understand her situation can also be beneficial. In cases where the partner's behavior does not change, it might be necessary to consider setting boundaries or seeking a safe environment to protect her well-being.

Understanding Emotional Shutdown in ADHD RSD

Emotional shutdown is a state where a person becomes emotionally numb or disconnected as a response to overwhelming stress or emotional pain. For a woman with ADHD and Rejection Sensitive Dysphoria (RSD), this phenomenon can be particularly pronounced and complex. Here's a detailed explanation of what emotional shutdown is, why it occurs, and its implications:

What is Emotional Shutdown?

Emotional shutdown is a protective mechanism where a person temporarily withdraws from or numbs their emotional responses. This can manifest as an inability to express emotions, difficulty in articulating thoughts, or a complete disengagement from emotional experiences. It often occurs when an individual is faced with overwhelming or unbearable emotional stress, leading them to shut down to avoid further emotional harm.

Reasons Behind Emotional Shutdown for an ADHD RSD Woman

1. **Overwhelming Emotional Sensitivity:**
    - **RSD and Intense Reactions**: People with ADHD and RSD are highly sensitive to rejection and criticism. When faced with harsh feedback or perceived rejection, the emotional response can be extreme. The intensity of these emotions can become too overwhelming, leading the individual to shut down as a means of coping with the emotional flood.
1. **Fear of Further Harm:**

- Narcissistic Behavior: If the partner exhibits narcissistic traits and continuously berates or insults her, she may fear that any attempt to respond or defend herself will only lead to more severe attacks. To protect herself from further emotional harm, she might withdraw and shut down.

1. **Inability to Process Emotionally Charged Situations:**
   - **Emotional Overload**: During high-conflict situations or when receiving repeated negative feedback, the emotional load can exceed her ability to process effectively. This overload can trigger a shutdown response where her brain essentially goes into survival mode, prioritizing emotional numbness over processing.

1. **Previous Trauma and Conditioning:**
   - **Past Experiences**: Previous experiences of emotional trauma or abuse can condition someone to shut down in response to conflict or criticism. If she has experienced similar patterns in the past, her brain might automatically revert to a shutdown state as a learned response to protect against perceived threats.

1. **Difficulty with Emotional Regulation**:
   - **ADHD and Emotional Regulation**: ADHD can affect a person's ability to regulate their emotions. Combined with RSD, which amplifies sensitivity to rejection, the person may struggle to manage and moderate their emotional responses, leading to shutdown when emotions become too intense or unmanageable.
1. **Perceived Ineffectiveness of Communication**:
   - **Fear of Misunderstanding**: If previous attempts to communicate have led to more conflict or misunderstanding, she may shut down due to the belief that expressing her feelings will be futile or will worsen the situation. This belief can reinforce the cycle of shutdown behavior.
1. **Psychological Exhaustion**:
   - **Constant Stress**: Ongoing emotional stress and strain can lead to psychological exhaustion. When someone is continually exposed to high levels of stress and emotional pain, their coping mechanisms can become depleted, leading to shutdown as a way to conserve emotional energy.

Implications of Emotional Shutdown

- **Communication Breakdown**: Emotional shutdown can lead to difficulties in communicating needs and feelings, further straining relationships and preventing resolution of conflicts.

- **Increased Isolation**: The inability to connect emotionally can contribute to feelings of isolation and loneliness, as the person may withdraw from social interactions and support networks.

- **Impact on Mental Health**: Prolonged emotional shutdown can contribute to mental health issues such as depression and anxiety, as the individual may feel disconnected from their emotions and unable to address underlying issues.

- **Impaired Self-Esteem**: Continual shutdown in response to criticism or rejection can erode self-esteem, as the person may internalize negative messages and feel inadequate or unworthy.

Addressing Emotional Shutdown

To address and mitigate emotional shutdown, it's important for the individual to seek support from mental health professionals who understand ADHD and RSD. Techniques such as therapy, mindfulness practices, and emotional regulation strategies can help in processing emotions and developing healthier coping mechanisms. Building a supportive environment with empathetic individuals can also provide a safe space for emotional expression and healing.

Pushing someone who has emotionally shut down is unproductive for several key reasons:

1. Overwhelms Emotional Capacity

When a person is in an emotional shutdown state, their capacity to process and respond to emotional stimuli is severely diminished. Continuing to push or pressure them can exacerbate their emotional overload, making it even harder for them to re-engage or articulate their feelings. Instead of facilitating resolution, it often leads to further emotional numbing and resistance.

2. Triggers Defensive Mechanisms

For individuals who have shut down, pushing them can trigger defensive mechanisms, such as heightened anxiety, increased stress, or further withdrawal. These defenses are often unconscious and are meant to protect the person from perceived threats or overwhelming feelings. When these defenses are activated, it becomes even more challenging for the person to engage in meaningful communication or emotional processing.

3. **Breaks Down Trust and Connection**

Pushing someone who is emotionally shut down can damage trust and strain the relationship. It can be perceived as invalidation or disregard for their emotional state, which can erode the sense of safety needed to open up. This can lead to increased feelings of isolation and a breakdown in the connection between the individual and those pushing them.

4. **Prevents Effective Communication**

Effective communication requires a level of emotional receptivity and openness. When someone has shut down, their ability to communicate is compromised. Pressing them to respond or share before they are ready can lead to ineffective communication or misunderstandings. The focus shifts from resolving the issue to managing the immediate emotional distress, which does not address the root cause of the shutdown.

5. **Increases Emotional Pain**

Pushing someone who has shut down can inadvertently increase their emotional pain. It can feel like an additional attack or stressor, compounding their existing emotional difficulties. This can result in a cycle of heightened emotional pain and further shutdown, rather than providing relief or resolution.

6. Disregards the Need for Self-Preservation

Emotional shutdown is often a self-preservation mechanism. It represents a person's attempt to protect themselves from emotional harm. Forcing someone to confront their emotions before they are ready disregards this protective mechanism and can be counterproductive, leading to increased emotional distress or resistance.

7. Impedes Healing and Recovery

Healing from emotional distress often requires time and a supportive environment. Pushing someone who has shut down can disrupt the natural process of healing and recovery. Instead of allowing the person to gradually regain their emotional equilibrium, pushing accelerates the process, which can be detrimental to their overall well-being.

8. **Fails to Address Underlying Issues**

Pushing for immediate responses or engagement does not address the underlying issues that led to the emotional shutdown. It focuses on surface-level interactions rather than exploring and resolving the deeper emotional or psychological issues at play. This can prevent meaningful progress and resolution of the core problems.

9. **May Lead to Conflict Escalation**

Pressuring someone who has shut down can escalate conflict rather than resolve it. The person may react defensively or with increased emotional intensity, which can exacerbate the situation and create more significant issues in the relationship.

10. **Undermines Autonomy and Respect**

Respecting an individual's need for space and time to process their emotions is crucial for maintaining healthy relationships. Pushing someone who is emotionally shut down undermines their autonomy and fails to honor their need for emotional self-regulation. This lack of respect can further damage the relationship and hinder emotional healing.

Alternative Approaches

- **Provide Space and Support**: Allow the individual time and space to process their emotions at their own pace. Offer support and understanding without pushing for immediate responses or engagement.
- **Use Empathy and Validation**: Express empathy and validate their feelings without pressuring them to talk or act before they are ready. Acknowledge their emotional state and reassure them that you are there for them.
- **Encourage Professional Help**: Suggest seeking support from mental health professionals who can help them navigate their emotional challenges in a safe and constructive manner.

By adopting these alternative approaches, you can create a supportive environment that respects the individual's emotional needs and fosters effective communication and healing.

A person who has experienced emotional shutdown and trauma, especially someone with ADHD and Rejection Sensitive Dysphoria (RSD), may avoid addressing issues

or having conversations about the problem for several reasons:

1. Fear of Escalation

If past experiences have taught them that addressing issues leads to escalation or worsening of the conflict, they may avoid the conversation to prevent additional pain. The anticipation of a heated argument or further emotional distress can make the prospect of discussing the problem seem unbearable.

2. Emotional Overwhelm

Emotional shutdown often occurs as a response to being overwhelmed. The idea of addressing a problem can feel like an additional stressor that they are not equipped to handle at the moment. They may avoid conversations because they feel emotionally depleted and fear that discussing the issue will push them beyond their current capacity.

3. Previous Negative Experiences

If they have had negative experiences in the past where attempts to address issues resulted in personal attacks, blame, or increased emotional pain, they may be reluctant to revisit those conversations. The fear of repeating past mistakes can lead to avoidance.

4. Fear of Rejection

Given that RSD involves heightened sensitivity to rejection and criticism, the person might fear that addressing the issue will lead to further rejection or criticism. This fear can be paralyzing, making them reluctant to initiate or engage in difficult conversations.

5. Lack of Trust

If the person has experienced repeated emotional harm from the other party, they may have lost trust in their ability to handle sensitive conversations constructively. A lack of trust in the other person's empathy or willingness to understand can lead them to avoid discussing the issues altogether.

6. Self-Protection

Avoiding the conversation can be a way of self-protection. If discussing the issue feels too risky or could result in further emotional damage, the person might choose to avoid it as a form of self-preservation. They may believe that not addressing the issue is a way to shield themselves from additional pain.

7. Inadequate Coping Skills

The person may lack the coping skills or strategies needed to navigate difficult conversations effectively. Without these skills, they might feel helpless or unequipped to handle the situation, leading them to avoid it rather than risk feeling more overwhelmed.

8. Avoidance of Vulnerability

Addressing sensitive issues often requires vulnerability and openness. For someone with RSD and emotional shutdown, this can be especially challenging. The fear of being vulnerable and exposing their emotional pain can lead them to avoid the conversation.

9. Perceived Futility

They might perceive that addressing the issue will not lead to a meaningful resolution or change. If they believe that past attempts to resolve similar issues have been unsuccessful, they might avoid the conversation, thinking it will only lead to further frustration or disappointment.

10. Difficulty Articulating Feelings

Emotional shutdown can make it challenging for individuals to articulate their feelings or thoughts clearly. The difficulty in expressing themselves can lead them to avoid conversations, as they may fear not being able to communicate their emotions effectively or being misunderstood.

11. Avoiding Conflict

For some, the idea of conflict is inherently stressful and anxiety-provoking. They may avoid conversations to sidestep the discomfort associated with conflict or confrontation. The avoidance serves as a temporary relief from the anticipated stress of engaging in a difficult discussion.

12. Coping Mechanism

Avoidance can be a coping mechanism to manage overwhelming emotions. By not addressing the issue, they may temporarily avoid the immediate distress but at the cost of unresolved problems that can fester and cause further emotional strain in the long run.

13. Expectations of Misunderstanding

If they anticipate that the other person will not understand their perspective or will react negatively, they might avoid the conversation to prevent the pain of being misunderstood or invalidated.

Alternative Approaches:

- **Seek Professional Guidance**: Engaging with a therapist or counselor can help the person develop effective strategies for addressing difficult issues and improving communication.
- **Build Communication Skills**: Learning and practicing effective communication skills can make it easier to address sensitive topics in a constructive manner.
- **Create a Safe Environment**: Establishing a safe and supportive environment for discussions can reduce the fear of negative outcomes and increase the likelihood of a productive conversation.

By understanding these reasons, it becomes clearer why someone might avoid addressing issues and how they can be supported in overcoming these challenges.

For a woman with ADHD and Rejection Sensitive Dysphoria (RSD), the emotional impact of being repeatedly told she is awful during an RSD episode can be profound and long-lasting. Here's an explanation of why she may struggle to let go of these negative perceptions:

1. **Deep-Seated Sensitivity to Rejection**

ADHD with RSD involves a heightened sensitivity to perceived rejection or criticism. When someone with RSD is told they are awful, these comments are not merely taken at face value but are deeply internalized. The brain of someone with RSD often processes these negative inputs as more significant and personally damaging than they might for others. This sensitivity can make it nearly impossible for them to dismiss or forget such criticisms.

2. **Internalization of Criticism**

The feedback received during an RSD episode can be internalized as an accurate reflection of their worth or identity. When repeatedly told they are awful, the individual might begin to believe this is their true self, especially if there's a lack of positive reinforcement or repair from the other person. This internalization means that even after the episode ends, the individual may continue to believe in the validity of the criticism and see it as a lasting judgment on their character.

3. Lack of Validation and Repair

For someone with RSD, the process of emotional healing is significantly impacted by the absence of validation or attempts at repairing the damage caused. If the other person fails to acknowledge their hurtful behavior or blames the RSD individual for their actions, it can reinforce the belief that the criticism was justified. Without validation and genuine efforts to make amends, the woman might perceive the other person's actions as further evidence of their disdain and negative feelings toward her.

4. Perceived Lack of Empathy

If the other person does not believe their behavior caused emotional pain or denies the impact of their actions, the RSD individual may feel invalidated and rejected. The lack of empathy or acknowledgment can deepen the belief that the negative views expressed are genuine. This reinforces their internal narrative that they are inherently flawed and disliked, making it harder to let go of the hurtful comments.

5. **Fear of Rejection and Self-Doubt**

When someone with RSD experiences criticism, it can trigger intense self-doubt and fear of rejection. If these feelings are not addressed or if the person does not receive reassurance and positive feedback, the fear of being rejected or unloved can become overwhelming. This ongoing fear can cause them to cling to the negative views expressed during the episode as a way to make sense of their emotional experience.

6. **Emotional Resonance**

The emotional resonance of hurtful comments during an RSD episode can be profound. For someone with RSD, the pain associated with these comments is often magnified, making it challenging to simply "let go" or move past the experience. The emotional intensity of the criticism can create a lasting impact that overshadows any subsequent attempts to reconcile or repair the relationship.

7. **Difficulty with Cognitive Flexibility**

ADHD often involves challenges with cognitive flexibility, which can make it difficult for individuals to shift their thinking or perspective. Once a negative belief is established, it may be challenging for them to reframe or let go of it, particularly when the belief is reinforced by ongoing negative interactions.

8. Confirmation Bias

People with RSD may experience confirmation bias, where they selectively focus on and remember instances that confirm their negative beliefs about themselves. If they have been repeatedly told they are awful, they may subconsciously seek out and emphasize evidence that supports this view, further entrenching the negative belief.

9. Impact on Self-Worth

The repeated negative feedback and lack of acknowledgment or repair can deeply impact their sense of self-worth. If someone with RSD feels that they are continuously criticized without any effort from the other person to mend the relationship, they may come to believe that the criticism reflects their true value and that they are unworthy of love or respect.

10. Emotional Scar Tissue

The emotional scars left by repeated negative experiences can make it difficult for someone with RSD to move on from past hurts. The cumulative effect of these experiences can create a sense of enduring emotional pain that colors their perception of current and future interactions.

Summary

In summary, for a woman with ADHD and RSD, the inability to let go of being told she is awful is rooted in the deep sensitivity to rejection, internalization of criticism, lack of validation, and perceived lack of empathy from the other person. The emotional impact of these experiences, combined with cognitive and emotional challenges, can make it incredibly difficult to move past such negative perceptions. This ongoing struggle highlights the need for empathy, validation, and effective communication to support someone with RSD in managing and healing from these intense emotional experiences.

The Brain's Focus on Negativity

For individuals with ADHD and RSD, the brain's heightened sensitivity to perceived rejection and criticism is not a matter of choice but a function of its design and wiring. This sensitivity means that negative experiences and emotional traumas can be disproportionately impactful, often overshadowing positive experiences or constructive feedback. When an individual with ADHD and RSD encounters verbal or emotional abuse, their brain processes these negative stimuli intensely, reinforcing the impact of the trauma.

Emotional Trauma and PTSD

Emotional trauma occurs when an individual experiences significant distress or harm, often due to events that challenge their emotional resilience or sense of safety. For those with ADHD and RSD, even seemingly minor negative interactions can be perceived as major threats due to their heightened sensitivity. This can lead to a more profound and lasting impact on their emotional well-being.

1. **Emotional Resonance**: The brain of someone with ADHD and RSD may resonate strongly with negative experiences. When exposed to verbal and emotional

abuse, the trauma is not only processed intensely but can also trigger a cascade of emotional responses reminiscent of past trauma. This creates a strong association between the abuse and the emotional pain experienced during the trauma, making it difficult to distinguish between past and present distress.

2. **Increased Vulnerability to PTSD**: Due to their heightened emotional sensitivity, individuals with ADHD and RSD are more susceptible to developing PTSD in response to verbal and emotional abuse. The intensity of their reactions can lead to the re-experiencing of trauma symptoms, such as flashbacks, intrusive thoughts, and heightened emotional arousal, which are characteristic of PTSD.

3. **Triggers and Flashbacks**: Verbal and emotional abuse can act as powerful triggers for individuals with ADHD and RSD. Certain tones of voice, yelling, or negative remarks can evoke memories of past trauma, causing the individual to relive the emotional pain associated with those experiences. This reliving of trauma can result in flashbacks or intense emotional responses,

reinforcing the cycle of trauma and emotional distress.

4. **Impact on Emotional Regulation**: ADHD and RSD can impair an individual's ability to regulate their emotions effectively. When faced with verbal and emotional abuse, the emotional dysregulation can exacerbate the impact of the trauma, making it more challenging to cope and recover. The emotional dysregulation can also contribute to heightened vulnerability to PTSD symptoms.

5. **Negative Self-Perception**: Verbal and emotional abuse can reinforce negative self-perceptions and beliefs, particularly for those with ADHD and RSD. The continuous reinforcement of negative feedback can lead to a persistent sense of worthlessness or inadequacy, which further contributes to the development of PTSD and chronic emotional distress.

6. **Difficulty in Processing Trauma**: Individuals with ADHD and RSD may struggle with processing and integrating traumatic experiences due to their heightened sensitivity and emotional reactivity. This difficulty in processing trauma can lead to unresolved

emotional issues and a greater likelihood of developing PTSD symptoms over time.

Conclusion

In summary, the brain of someone with ADHD and RSD is particularly sensitive to negativity, which can make them more susceptible to the effects of emotional trauma and verbal abuse. This heightened sensitivity can exacerbate the impact of such abuse, leading to symptoms consistent with PTSD. The emotional pain experienced during episodes of verbal and emotional abuse can deeply affect their sense of self and well-being, creating a cycle of trauma that is challenging to break. Understanding this connection emphasizes the importance of providing support and validation to individuals with ADHD and RSD to help them manage and recover from trauma and its effects.

The constant feeling of shame and embarrassment can be particularly overwhelming for someone with ADHD and Rejection Sensitive Dysphoria (RSD). These emotions often stem from a deep-seated fear of judgment and a pervasive sense of inadequacy, and they can significantly impact a person's mental and emotional well-being.

Here's an in-depth look at how these feelings manifest and their effects:

Understanding Constant Shame and Embarrassment

1. **Origins of Shame and Embarrassment**:
   - **Rejection Sensitivity**: For individuals with RSD, even minor rejections or perceived failures can trigger intense feelings of shame and embarrassment. These reactions are often disproportionate to the actual event, driven by the heightened emotional sensitivity characteristic of RSD.
   - **Negative Self-Perception**: Continuous experiences of criticism, failure, or negative feedback can contribute to a persistent negative self-image. This self-perception can become internalized, leading to feelings of shame and embarrassment about one's abilities or worth.

1. **Emotional Impact**:
   - **Persistent Self-Criticism**: The individual may engage in harsh self-criticism, constantly berating themselves for perceived shortcomings or

mistakes. This internal dialogue reinforces feelings of inadequacy and perpetuates a cycle of shame.

- **Fear of Exposure**: Shame often involves a fear of being exposed or judged by others. The person may feel vulnerable and anxious about revealing their true self, leading to avoidance of social situations or opportunities where they might face potential judgment.

- **Social Withdrawal**: To avoid the risk of further embarrassment, the individual may withdraw from social interactions or avoid situations where they could potentially experience shame. This withdrawal can lead to isolation and further exacerbate feelings of loneliness and inadequacy.

1. **Psychological Consequences**:

- **Impaired Self-Esteem**: Constant feelings of shame and embarrassment can severely impact self-esteem. The person may struggle with self-worth, feeling undeserving of success or happiness due to their perceived flaws.

- **Increased Anxiety and Depression**: Persistent shame can contribute to heightened anxiety and depressive symptoms. The emotional burden of feeling flawed or inadequate can lead to chronic stress, affecting overall mental health and well-being.

- ○ **Difficulty in Self-Acceptance**: The inability to accept oneself due to ongoing shame can hinder personal growth and self-compassion. The person may struggle to recognize and celebrate their strengths and achievements, focusing instead on their perceived failings.

DIFFICULT BUT CAN BE DONE

Maintaining steady self-esteem can be challenging for adults with ADHD, but it's definitely achievable with the right strategies and mindset. Building and sustaining self-esteem for someone with ADHD involves self-acceptance, recognizing their strengths, reframing negative thoughts, and developing systems that support emotional regulation. Here's how they can get and keep steady self-esteem:

1. Self-Awareness and Acceptance

Self-esteem starts with accepting yourself for who you are, including your ADHD traits. This involves understanding how ADHD impacts your life, acknowledging your struggles, and embracing the positive aspects of your unique brain wiring.

- **How to do it**:
  - **Educate yourself**: Learn about ADHD from reputable sources, books, and communities. Understanding your condition allows you to frame your struggles as part of your neurobiology, not as personal failings.
  - **Acknowledge strengths**: ADHD comes with many strengths, such as creativity, problem-solving abilities, and hyperfocus. Make a conscious effort to identify and celebrate these traits.
  - **Reframe challenges**: Instead of viewing ADHD-related difficulties as flaws, reframe them as traits that simply need different approaches to manage. For example, impulsivity can be seen as spontaneity and adaptability when channeled productively.
- **Why it helps**: When you accept yourself, flaws and all, it becomes harder for external criticism to erode your

self-worth. Self-awareness allows you to stop comparing yourself to neurotypical standards and embrace your unique way of functioning.

2. **Develop Self-Compassion**

People with ADHD tend to be their own worst critics, which can lower self-esteem. Practicing self-compassion means treating yourself with the same kindness and understanding that you would offer to a close friend.

- **How to do it**:
    - **Talk to yourself kindly**: When you make mistakes, avoid harsh self-criticism. Instead, tell yourself, "It's okay, everyone makes mistakes," or "I'm doing the best I can with what I have."
    - **Forgive yourself for slip-ups**: ADHD involves inconsistency. Instead of dwelling on bad days or moments of forgetfulness, remind yourself that perfection isn't possible, and it's okay to have setbacks.
    - **Practice mindfulness**: Mindfulness exercises can help you become more aware of your negative self-talk and emotional reactions. Through

mindfulness, you can interrupt the cycle of self-criticism and replace it with self-compassion.

- **Why it helps**: Self-compassion allows you to bounce back from failures or criticism without letting them affect your overall sense of self-worth. Over time, it builds resilience against external negativity.

3. **Set Realistic Goals and Expectations**

People with ADHD often set overly ambitious or perfectionistic goals, which can lead to disappointment and self-criticism when they aren't achieved. Creating realistic, attainable goals will help stabilize self-esteem by ensuring more consistent feelings of accomplishment.

- **How to do it**:
  - **Break goals into smaller steps**: Instead of aiming for large, all-or-nothing goals, break them into manageable steps. Each step completed can boost your confidence and reinforce a sense of progress.
  - **Celebrate small victories**: Acknowledge and reward yourself for small accomplishments, like finishing a task on time or managing your schedule

effectively. Even small wins matter when building self-esteem.

- ○ **Adjust expectations**: Understand that ADHD comes with certain challenges, such as fluctuating focus and energy. Set expectations that align with your capabilities on any given day, and be flexible when things don't go as planned.

☐ **Why it helps**: Realistic goals help you build confidence gradually, and small wins reinforce a sense of competence. This process minimizes the chances of feeling overwhelmed or defeated.

4. Create Supportive Structures

ADHD can create chaos and disorganization, which often leads to feelings of inadequacy. Setting up systems that help manage ADHD symptoms can reduce stress and build a sense of control and competence.

- **How to do it**:
  - ○ **Use external tools**: Set up reminders, alarms, and calendars to stay on track. Breaking down tasks into clear lists or using productivity apps can help organize your time and reduce forgetfulness.

- Seek accountability: Share your goals or plans
  with trusted friends, family members, or a coach.
  Accountability can help you stay on track and
  provide external validation when needed.
- Create ADHD-friendly routines: Structure your
  day in a way that works for your brain. For
  example, do more demanding tasks during times
  when you feel most alert, and schedule breaks to
  prevent burnout.

- **Why it helps**: ADHD-friendly systems and routines
  help minimize forgetfulness and inconsistency, which
  can often cause self-doubt. When you're able to
  manage your responsibilities better, your self-esteem
  is less likely to take a hit.

5. Cognitive Restructuring: Challenge Negative Thoughts

Many people with ADHD develop negative self-beliefs
from years of criticism, disappointment, or comparison
to others. Cognitive restructuring involves identifying
and challenging these negative thoughts, so they don't
undermine your self-esteem.

- **How to do it**:

- **Identify negative beliefs**: Pay attention to recurring negative thoughts like "I'm lazy" or "I'll never get things right." Write them down.
- **Challenge those thoughts**: Ask yourself if these thoughts are really true. Look for evidence to the contrary times when you were hardworking, capable, or successful.
- **Replace with positive affirmations**: Reframe the negative thoughts into more balanced, compassionate statements. For example, instead of "I'm so disorganized," tell yourself, "I have challenges with organization, but I'm working on improving it."

- **Why it helps**: Over time, reprogramming your brain to focus on positive and realistic thoughts instead of harsh criticisms will help you build a more stable sense of self-worth.

6. Surround Yourself with Supportive People

Your environment has a significant impact on self-esteem. Being around people who are supportive, understanding, and non-judgmental can boost your confidence, while toxic relationships can erode it.

- **How to do it**:
  - Seek ADHD communities: Engage with online or in-person ADHD support groups. Being around others who understand your struggles can make you feel validated and less alone.
  - **Build a positive network**: Surround yourself with friends and loved ones who appreciate your unique qualities, provide encouragement, and are patient with your ADHD traits.
  - **Distance yourself from toxic influences**: If certain people in your life are consistently critical, unsupportive, or dismissive of your ADHD, it may be necessary to set boundaries to protect your self-esteem.
- **Why it helps**: Positive reinforcement from others helps counteract self-doubt and
- feelings of inadequacy. Supportive relationships provide a buffer against the negative
- messages that can come from both internal and external sources.

7. Develop Emotional Regulation Skills

ADHD often leads to heightened emotional responses, especially to criticism or failure. Learning emotional regulation skills can help stabilize self-esteem by preventing you from overreacting to setbacks or negative feedback.

- **How to do it**:
  - **Practice mindfulness and meditation**: These techniques can help you become more aware of your emotional triggers and give you the tools to manage them before they spiral out of control.
  - **Deep breathing and grounding exercises**: When faced with criticism or a challenging situation, take a moment to breathe deeply and ground yourself in the present moment. This helps prevent an emotional flood that can damage your self-esteem.
  - **Cognitive Behavioral Therapy (CBT)**: CBT techniques can help you identify and change the thought patterns that lead to emotional dysregulation. Working with a therapist to develop these skills can be highly effective.
- **Why it helps**: Emotional regulation prevents small setbacks from turning into major
- self-esteem crises. By keeping emotions in check, you maintain a balanced sense of

- self-worth, even when things don't go perfectly.

8. **Focus on Strength-Based Living**

ADHD doesn't just come with challenges; it also comes with unique strengths. Building your life around your strengths—whether it's creativity, problem-solving, or hyperfocus—can boost your self-esteem by allowing you to shine in areas where you excel.

- **How to do it**:
  - **Identify your strengths**: Make a list of areas where you naturally excel. This could be creative thinking, adaptability, empathy, or the ability to focus intensely on tasks that interest you.
  - **Lean into these strengths**: Build your career, hobbies, or personal life around these strengths. For example, if you're great at brainstorming but struggle with details, find ways to focus on big-picture tasks while delegating or seeking help with smaller tasks.
  - **Get feedback on your strengths**: Ask others what they think you're good at. Sometimes, hearing positive feedback from an outside perspective can reinforce your confidence in those areas.

- **Why it helps**: By focusing on what you do well, you're constantly reinforcing the message that you are capable and talented. This can counterbalance any negativity from ADHD-related struggles.

Maintaining steady self-esteem as an adult with ADHD involves a combination of self-awareness, self-compassion, realistic goal setting, supportive environments, emotional regulation, and focusing on strengths. By embracing your ADHD traits, reframing negative thoughts, and building systems that support your well-being, you can protect and sustain your self-esteem over time.

SELF-AWARENESS

Self-awareness is crucial for individuals with ADHD and Rejection Sensitive Dysphoria (RSD) because it provides a foundation for understanding, managing, and mitigating the impact of their emotional and cognitive experiences. Here's why self-awareness is particularly important:

**1. Recognizing Triggers:

For people with ADHD and RSD, specific situations, comments, or interactions can trigger intense emotional responses. Self-awareness helps them identify what triggers their RSD episodes. By understanding these triggers, individuals can anticipate and prepare for potential emotional challenges, reducing the likelihood of being caught off guard.

**2. Understanding Emotional Responses:

Self-awareness allows individuals to differentiate between their actual feelings and their automatic emotional reactions. People with RSD may experience heightened emotional responses that are disproportionate to the situation. Being aware of this can help them recognize when their feelings are being amplified by RSD rather than being a direct reflection of the actual situation.

**3. Developing Coping Strategies:

Once individuals become aware of their emotional patterns and triggers, they can develop targeted coping strategies. For example, recognizing that certain types of feedback or social interactions tend to trigger RSD can help them implement strategies like taking deep breaths, using affirmations, or engaging in calming activities to manage their reactions.

**4. Improving Communication:

Self-awareness enhances an individual's ability to communicate their needs and feelings effectively. Understanding how RSD affects their reactions and emotions enables them to express their needs to others more clearly. This can lead to better support from friends, family, and colleagues, and reduce misunderstandings.

**5. Building Resilience:

By being aware of their emotional responses and patterns, individuals can build resilience against RSD. Self-awareness helps them recognize when they are in the midst of an RSD episode and use coping strategies more effectively. This resilience can lead to improved emotional regulation and a better ability to handle future stressors.

**6. Enhancing Self-Esteem:

Self-awareness can also contribute to healthier self-esteem. Understanding that their intense emotional responses are part of their ADHD and RSD, rather than a reflection of personal inadequacy, helps individuals be kinder to themselves. This self-compassion can mitigate the negative impact on their self-esteem and foster a more balanced self-view.

**7. Facilitating Personal Growth:

Self-awareness promotes personal growth by encouraging individuals to reflect on their behaviors, reactions, and thought patterns. It helps them recognize areas where they can improve and work towards changing maladaptive patterns. This ongoing self-reflection can lead to personal development and greater emotional well-being.

**8. Managing Relationships:

In relationships, self-awareness helps individuals with ADHD and RSD communicate more effectively and manage conflicts better. By understanding how their RSD affects their interactions, they can work on improving their relational skills, setting boundaries, and fostering healthier, more supportive relationships.

**9. Promoting Emotional Health:

Self-awareness supports overall emotional health by enabling individuals to understand their emotional needs and responses. This understanding helps in managing anxiety, depression, and other emotional challenges often associated with ADHD and RSD. It promotes proactive mental health management and reduces the likelihood of emotional overwhelm.

10. **Empowering Decision-Making:

With greater self-awareness, individuals are better equipped to make informed decisions about their lives. They can assess how their emotional responses might influence their choices and actions, leading to more deliberate and thoughtful decision-making processes.

In Summary:

Self-awareness serves as a foundational skill for managing ADHD and RSD. It enables individuals to recognize and understand their emotional responses, anticipate and mitigate triggers, communicate effectively, and develop coping strategies. By fostering self-awareness, individuals with ADHD and RSD can navigate their emotional landscape more effectively, leading to improved emotional regulation, healthier relationships, and overall well-being.

Building self-awareness and self-acceptance is a Must

Building self-awareness and self-acceptance is essential for personal growth, emotional well-being, and maintaining healthy self-esteem, especially for individuals with ADHD. It helps you better understand your thoughts, feelings, and behaviors, allowing you to make more intentional decisions. Here are **20 ways to build self-awareness and self-acceptance**:

1. Practice Mindfulness

Mindfulness involves paying attention to the present moment without judgment. It helps you become more aware of your thoughts, feelings, and bodily sensations, which can reveal patterns of behavior and emotions that you might otherwise overlook.

- **How to do it**: Spend 5-10 minutes daily in mindful meditation, focusing on your breath or observing your thoughts as they arise without getting attached to them.

2. Keep a Daily Journal

Journaling allows you to reflect on your experiences, emotions, and thoughts. It can reveal patterns in your thinking and behavior that contribute to stress, self-doubt, or low self-esteem.

- **How to do it**: Write about your feelings, experiences, and reactions at the end of each day, paying attention to what made you feel good or bad.

3. Take Personality Assessments

Tools like the Myers-Briggs Type Indicator (MBTI), Enneagram, or StrengthsFinder can offer insights into your personality traits, helping you understand your strengths and areas for growth.

- **How to do it**: Find credible online assessments or books that explain different personality types and apply them to your own experiences.

4. Reflect on Feedback from Others

Seeking feedback from trusted friends, family, or colleagues can provide valuable insights into how others perceive you. This external perspective can help you recognize blind spots in your behavior or communication.

- **How to do it**: Ask people close to you for honest feedback about your strengths, areas to improve, or how they see you handling certain situations.

5. Identify Emotional Triggers

Notice what situations, people, or thoughts trigger strong emotional reactions. Recognizing these triggers can help you understand unresolved issues or vulnerabilities.

Identifying emotional triggers, especially in individuals with ADHD and Rejection Sensitive Dysphoria (RSD), is an important step in managing overwhelming emotional responses. Emotional triggers are specific situations, people, or events that provoke strong negative feelings such as anger, sadness, anxiety, or shame. These reactions can feel disproportionate to the situation at hand because they tap into deeper unresolved emotions or past experiences. Here's how to identify emotional triggers effectively:

1. Track Emotional Responses

One of the most straightforward ways to identify emotional triggers is by paying close attention to moments when you experience intense emotional reactions. Keeping a journal or log of these events can help you detect patterns over time. Each time you experience a strong emotional reaction, ask yourself the following:

- What happened right before I started feeling this way?
- What thoughts went through my mind?
- How did my body respond (e.g., heart racing, tension, sweating)?
- What did I do in response to this feeling?

For example, you might notice that your heart races and you feel overwhelmed when your boss gives you feedback, even if the feedback is constructive. This could indicate that criticism is a trigger for you.

Journaling Example:

- Situation: A coworker suggested a small improvement to my project.
- Emotional Reaction: Felt immediate panic and anger, heart raced.
- Thoughts: "They think I'm incompetent."
- Physical Response: Tense muscles, shallow breathing.
- Behavioral Response: Became defensive and avoided the coworker.

Over time, similar entries may reveal that criticism or perceived inadequacies are major emotional triggers.

2. Reflect on Past Emotional Outbursts

Reflecting on past situations where you felt emotionally overwhelmed can give insight into common themes or patterns. Think about significant moments when you felt rejected, criticized, or vulnerable:

- Were there certain situations or people involved?
- Did the emotions feel more intense than the situation warranted?
- Were the emotions connected to past experiences, even if subconsciously?

For individuals with RSD, past experiences of rejection or failure can significantly influence present triggers. You may discover that certain environments, like a competitive workspace or social gatherings, consistently evoke these emotional responses because they mirror earlier negative experiences.

Reflection Example:

- Past Situation: As a teenager, I was publicly criticized by a teacher in front of the class, which was humiliating.

- Current Trigger: Whenever someone gives me feedback in front of others, I feel the same sense of embarrassment and shame, even when it's minor.

3. Observe Your Thought Patterns

Our thoughts often provide clues to our emotional triggers. Cognitive distortions, such as black-and-white thinking, catastrophizing, or assuming the worst, can amplify emotional responses. When triggered, individuals with RSD may have automatic negative thoughts like:

- "I'm worthless because I messed up."
- "They're going to leave me."
- "Everyone thinks I'm a failure."

Identifying recurring thought patterns can help you recognize your emotional triggers. For example, if you frequently think, "I'm not good enough," when you receive feedback, this thought pattern might be linked to your emotional trigger of criticism or judgment.

Thought Pattern Example:

- Trigger: A friend doesn't respond to a text message immediately.
- Automatic Thought: "They don't want to be friends anymore."

- Emotional Reaction: Panic, insecurity, and fear of abandonment.

Once you're aware of these thoughts, you can challenge and reframe them, which can help diffuse the emotional trigger.

4. Identify Physical Sensations

Emotional triggers often manifest physically before we are consciously aware of the emotional response. Paying attention to physical sensations can help you identify when you are being triggered. These may include:

- Increased heart rate or pounding heart
- Sweaty palms
- Tension in muscles, especially in the neck and shoulders
- Shallow or rapid breathing
- Nausea or a sinking feeling in the stomach

By noting your physical responses, you can become more attuned to the early warning signs of an emotional trigger. For example, you might notice that your chest tightens and your palms get sweaty right before a wave of anger hits, which could indicate that your fight-or-flight response is being activated.

Physical Sensation Example:

- Situation: Receiving a critical email from a colleague.
- Physical Sensation: Tightness in my chest and shortness of breath.
- Emotional Reaction: Feeling disrespected and angry.
- Behavioral Response: Rushed to respond defensively without fully reading the email.

5. Explore Core Beliefs

Core beliefs are deeply held assumptions about yourself, others, and the world. They often stem from childhood experiences or significant past events and can serve as the foundation for emotional triggers. Common core beliefs among people with RSD may include:

- "I'm unlovable."
- "I'll never be good enough."
- "People will always reject me."

These core beliefs can act as the root cause of emotional triggers, as certain situations reinforce these deeply held fears. For instance, if you believe you're not good enough, even a minor critique might feel like confirmation of this belief, triggering an emotional reaction.

Core Belief Example:

- Belief: "I'm not capable of success."
- Trigger: Receiving feedback that a project needs improvement.
- Emotional Reaction: Feeling devastated, as though the feedback confirms that I'll never succeed.
- Behavioral Response: Procrastinating or avoiding future projects to prevent failure.

By identifying your core beliefs, you can work on challenging and changing them, which reduces the power of emotional triggers.

6. Notice Social Dynamics

Social interactions are often a source of emotional triggers for people with RSD. Situations that involve relationships, group dynamics, or feelings of inclusion and exclusion can be particularly sensitive. If you often feel rejected or anxious in social settings, take note of the specific dynamics that trigger your emotions:

- Do you feel anxious in large groups or when meeting new people?
- Are you more sensitive to feedback from certain individuals, such as authority figures or close friends?

- Does feeling left out or overlooked cause intense emotional responses?

For individuals with RSD, interactions that carry even a hint of rejection or exclusion can feel devastating. Learning to identify these social triggers can help you understand why certain interactions are more emotionally charged.

Social Trigger Example:

- Trigger: Not being invited to a social event that others in your group are attending.
- Emotional Reaction: Feeling devastated and like you don't belong.
- Thought: "They don't like me; I'm not important to them."
- Behavioral Response: Withdrawing from the group and avoiding future interactions.

7. Seek Feedback from Others

Sometimes, those close to you can provide valuable insights into your emotional triggers. Asking trusted friends, family members, or a therapist for their observations can help you see patterns that you may not be fully aware of. They may notice that you seem more reactive in certain situations or around specific people.

Feedback Example:

- Friend's Observation: "I notice you tend to shut down whenever someone disagrees with you in group discussions."
- Your Reflection: "I think disagreement makes me feel rejected and misunderstood, which is why I react that way."

8. Practice Self-Compassion

Understanding your emotional triggers can be challenging, as it often requires confronting painful memories or recognizing patterns of behavior that you'd rather avoid. Practicing self-compassion is key to navigating this process without judgment. Remind yourself that emotional triggers are a natural part of the human experience, and identifying them is the first step toward growth and healing.

Identifying emotional triggers is essential for managing emotional responses, especially for individuals with ADHD and RSD. By tracking emotional reactions, reflecting on past experiences, observing thought patterns and physical sensations, exploring core beliefs, and seeking feedback from trusted individuals, you can gain a deeper understanding of the specific situations that trigger your emotions. Recognizing these triggers allows you to develop healthier coping strategies and reduce the intensity of your emotional responses over time.

6. Explore Your Core Beliefs

core beliefs are deeply held convictions that influence how we interpret our experiences, view ourselves, and interact with the world around us. They often develop early in life and shape the lens through which we see our relationships, successes, failures, and even our self-worth. For individuals with ADHD, especially those experiencing Rejection Sensitive Dysphoria (RSD), core beliefs can play a crucial role in amplifying emotional responses to perceived rejection, criticism, or failure. Here's a breakdown of how core beliefs affect your self-perception and behaviors, and how understanding these beliefs can lead to self-growth.

How Core Beliefs are Formed

Core beliefs often stem from past experiences, particularly those in early childhood. They can be influenced by interactions with parents, teachers, friends, and authority figures, as well as significant life events such as trauma, academic challenges, or consistent criticism. For someone with ADHD, difficulties in school, social interactions, or constant comparisons to neurotypical peers can solidify negative beliefs about oneself.

Examples of Common Core Beliefs:

- **"I'm not good enough."**
- **"I don't deserve success."**
- **"People will always leave me."**
- **"I'm too much to handle."**

These core beliefs form a subconscious framework that influences how you interpret everyday situations. For instance, if you believe, "I'm not good enough," you may view a minor critique at work as confirmation of that belief, even if the critique was constructive and not intended to be personal.

The Impact of Core Beliefs on Self-Perception

Core beliefs are powerful because they are often internalized as absolute truths, and they can be difficult to recognize since they operate beneath the surface. They shape your internal narrative and impact your self-esteem, relationships, and decision-making.

How Core Beliefs Affect Self-Perception:

1. **Self-Criticism:** Negative core beliefs fuel harsh self-criticism. If your belief is, "I'm a failure," you'll likely focus on mistakes or shortcomings while disregarding achievements or progress. This can lead to feelings of inadequacy and constant anxiety about meeting expectations.

2. **Perfectionism:** Individuals with core beliefs like "I'm not good enough" may strive for perfection to counter these feelings. Perfectionism is often a coping mechanism to shield oneself from perceived judgment or rejection, but it can lead to burnout and stress, as the standard of "perfection" is unattainable.

3. **Imposter Syndrome:** Core beliefs such as "I don't deserve success" can manifest as imposter syndrome. Even in the face of accomplishments, you may feel like a fraud or believe that success was due to luck

rather than skill, which erodes confidence and fosters self-doubt.

4. **Avoidance of Challenges:** If you hold a belief like "I'll never succeed," you may avoid taking on new challenges or pursuing opportunities out of fear of failure. This avoidance reinforces the core belief because it prevents you from testing your abilities or experiencing growth through trial and error.

The Role of Core Beliefs in Emotional Reactions

For individuals with ADHD and RSD, core beliefs significantly influence emotional responses, especially in situations involving criticism, rejection, or failure. Since core beliefs act as filters for how we process information, they can intensify emotional reactions. When a core belief is triggered, the emotional response can be far more intense than the situation warrants, as the underlying fear or insecurity comes to the forefront.

Example of Emotional Triggering by Core Beliefs:

- **Core Belief:** "I'm not worthy of love."
- **Situation:** A friend cancels plans at the last minute.
- **Emotional Reaction:** Instead of recognizing that the friend may have legitimate reasons for canceling, you

feel deeply hurt and abandoned. Your core belief is triggered, leading you to think, "This always happens because I'm unlovable."

- **Resulting Behavior:** You withdraw emotionally or become overly defensive, reinforcing feelings of rejection.

In this scenario, the core belief has shaped your interpretation of the situation, magnifying the emotional impact. Over time, repeated triggering of these beliefs reinforces the cycle of negative self-perception and emotional distress.

Identifying and Challenging Core Beliefs

Identifying core beliefs requires introspection and a willingness to examine patterns in your thoughts, emotions, and behaviors. Here are steps you can take to uncover and challenge your core beliefs:

1. Notice Repeating Patterns

Start by paying attention to situations that evoke strong emotional responses. Are there common themes or triggers, such as criticism, rejection, or social interactions? Ask yourself:

- What is the recurring thought I have in these situations?
- Does this thought seem exaggerated or absolute?

For instance, if you frequently feel overwhelmed by social anxiety, you might find that the recurring thought is, "No one likes me," which reflects a core belief of unworthiness or rejection.

2. Examine the Origin of the Belief

Once you've identified a core belief, ask yourself where it came from. Core beliefs are often rooted in past experiences, particularly those from childhood or adolescence. Reflect on:

- When did I first start thinking this way?
- Who or what reinforced this belief in the past?

For example, if you believe, "I'm not good enough," it may stem from being compared to siblings or peers growing up, where you felt you couldn't meet expectations.

3. Challenge the Validity of the Belief

Core beliefs often feel like truths, but they are usually based on faulty logic or past experiences that no longer apply. To challenge a core belief, ask yourself:

- Is this belief always true, or are there exceptions?
- What evidence supports or contradicts this belief?
- How would someone else view this situation?

For instance, if you believe, "I'm always failing," consider times when you've succeeded or met your goals. It's crucial to gather evidence that counters the negative belief and provide a more balanced perspective.

4. Reframe the Belief

Once you've identified and challenged a core belief, work on reframing it into a healthier, more balanced thought. This doesn't mean replacing it with overly positive affirmations, but rather creating a belief that is rooted in reality and self-compassion.

Reframing Example:

- **Original Core Belief:** "I'm not good enough."
- **Reframed Belief:** "I'm capable of growth, and my worth isn't determined by one mistake."

This new belief allows room for imperfection and emphasizes progress rather than an unrealistic standard of perfection.

Impact of Changing Core Beliefs on Actions and Perspectives

Once you begin to challenge and change your core beliefs, you'll likely notice a shift in how you perceive yourself and interact with the world. When your beliefs become more compassionate and flexible, your actions will align with this newfound perspective. Some of the effects may include:

- **Improved Emotional Regulation:** By reframing core beliefs, you may experience less emotional intensity in situations that would have previously triggered you.
- **Increased Resilience:** A shift in core beliefs can help you become more resilient in the face of setbacks. You'll be better equipped to handle criticism or failure without internalizing it as a reflection of your worth.
- **Healthier Relationships:** Core beliefs like "I'm not lovable" can undermine relationships, leading to self-sabotage or withdrawal. By challenging these beliefs, you can foster healthier connections based on mutual respect and understanding.

Understanding your core beliefs is crucial for personal growth, especially for those with ADHD and RSD, where emotional sensitivity and self-criticism often run high. By identifying and challenging these beliefs, you can begin to transform how you view yourself, handle emotional triggers, and engage with the world around you. While changing core beliefs takes time and effort, it can lead to a more balanced, compassionate, and empowered life.

- **How to do it**: Reflect on what you believe about yourself, success, relationships, and life in general. Question whether these beliefs are helping or hindering your well-being.

7. Meditate on Self-Compassion

Self-compassion involves treating yourself with the same kindness you'd offer a close friend. Meditation can help you cultivate this compassion, leading to greater self-acceptance.

- **How to do it**: Use guided self-compassion meditations to practice kindness towards yourself, especially during moments of failure or difficulty.

8. Track Your Habits

By tracking daily habits—whether productive or unproductive—you become more aware of patterns in your behavior that may be helping or hindering your progress.

- **How to do it**: Use a habit-tracking app or a simple notebook to log your daily habits and routines. Reflect on which habits bring you closer to your goals and which ones create obstacles.

9. Challenge Negative Self-Talk

Often, we engage in automatic negative self-talk without realizing it. Becoming aware of these inner dialogues helps challenge harmful thought patterns and replace them with more positive ones.

- **How to do it**: When you catch yourself thinking negatively, pause and ask, "Is this thought true? What evidence do I have to support or challenge it?"

10. Embrace Imperfection

Perfectionism can create stress and self-criticism. Embracing your imperfections allows for more self-acceptance and resilience when things don't go as planned.

- **How to do it**: Practice letting go of the need to do things perfectly. Set realistic standards for yourself and acknowledge that mistakes are a part of growth.

11. Engage in Self-Reflection

Take time to think about your actions, decisions, and feelings. Reflecting on your behavior helps you understand why you react in certain ways and what you can do differently in the future.

- **How to do it**: At the end of the day or week, review significant events or interactions and ask yourself what you learned or could improve upon.

12. Set Personal Boundaries

Knowing your limits and setting boundaries is a crucial part of self-awareness. It helps you recognize when you're overextending yourself or compromising your values.

- **How to do it**: Identify situations where you feel drained or resentful. Practice saying no or setting clear boundaries to protect your emotional and mental well-being.

13. Work with a Therapist or Coach

A therapist or life coach can help you gain deeper insights into your behaviors, thought patterns, and emotional triggers. Professional guidance offers structured support for building self-awareness.

- **How to do it**: Consider working with a therapist specializing in ADHD or emotional well-being or hire a life coach to help you set and achieve personal development goals.

14. Monitor Your Emotional States

Track your emotional fluctuations throughout the day. Recognizing how different situations or people affect your mood can provide valuable insights into your emotional triggers and coping mechanisms.

- **How to do it**: Use a mood-tracking app or journal to log your emotional highs and lows. Look for patterns that can help you better manage your emotions.

15. Practice Gratitude

Focusing on what you're grateful for helps you shift attention from what's wrong to what's working well in your life. This practice can increase self-acceptance by recognizing the positive aspects of who you are.

- **How to do it**: Write down three things you're grateful for every day. Include personal qualities, achievements, or positive experiences.

16. Learn from Mistakes

Mistakes can provide valuable learning opportunities. Instead of beating yourself up, reflect on what went wrong, what you learned, and how you can apply that lesson moving forward.

- **How to do it**: After a mistake, ask yourself, "What can I learn from this?" Focus on growth and improvement rather than self-blame.

17. Develop a Growth Mindset

A growth mindset involves viewing challenges and setbacks as opportunities for growth rather than as failures. This mindset encourages self-acceptance by fostering resilience and adaptability.

- **How to do it**: When faced with a challenge, remind yourself that setbacks are a natural part of learning and improving. Focus on the process rather than the outcome.

18. Practice Emotional Honesty

Being honest with yourself about your feelings, rather than suppressing or ignoring them, is key to self-awareness. It allows you to understand your emotional needs and take appropriate actions.

- **How to do it**: When you're feeling emotional, name the feeling and accept it without judgment. Ask yourself why you feel that way and what you might need to address it.

19. **Recognize Your Accomplishments**

Acknowledging your achievements helps you see your strengths and abilities more clearly, building both self-awareness and self-acceptance.

- **How to do it**: Regularly review your successes, no matter how small, and take time to celebrate them. This reinforces your belief in your capabilities.

20. **Engage in Self-Care**

Self-care is about taking intentional actions to nurture your mental, emotional, and physical well-being. It promotes self-acceptance by reinforcing that you are worthy of care and attention.

- **How to do it**: Prioritize activities that rejuvenate you, such as exercise, hobbies, rest, or spending time with loved ones. Self-care reinforces the belief that you deserve kindness and attention.

Building self-awareness and acceptance is an ongoing process that requires patience and consistent effort. By practicing mindfulness, engaging in reflection, and being kind to yourself, you can cultivate a deeper understanding of your inner world. These 20 strategies provide a wide range of tools that can help you on your journey to self-awareness and acceptance, fostering a healthier relationship with yourself.

RSD HAS SIGNIFICANT IMPACT ON SELF ESTEEM

Yes, **Rejection Sensitive Dysphoria (RSD)** can have a significant impact on self-esteem, often without any clear or external reasons why. RSD is a common emotional experience in people with ADHD, where they feel intense emotional pain due to perceived rejection, criticism, or failure. Here's how RSD can contribute to low self-esteem, even when there might not be obvious reasons for it:

1. Perception of Rejection is Heightened

People with RSD often perceive rejection where it may not exist or overemphasize minor criticisms. This heightened sensitivity can make them feel like they are constantly being judged or rejected, even in neutral or supportive environments.

- **Impact on self-esteem**: When someone feels rejected repeatedly, it reinforces the belief that they are unworthy or not good enough, leading to low self-esteem. Even if these rejections are not real or significant, the emotional impact feels very real.

2. Overreaction to Criticism

With RSD, even mild or constructive criticism can feel overwhelming. The emotional response is so intense that it overshadows the actual content of the feedback.

- **Impact on self-esteem**: This overreaction can create a negative feedback loop where the person begins to see any form of critique as a personal failure, which erodes their confidence and self-worth over time.

3. Fear of Rejection

RSD often leads to an intense fear of rejection. This fear can cause someone to anticipate rejection in situations where none exists, causing them to withdraw or avoid challenges that could enhance their self-esteem.

- **Impact on self-esteem**: Avoidance behaviors limit opportunities for growth and positive reinforcement, leaving a person feeling stuck or inadequate. Over time, this can prevent someone from developing a strong sense of self-worth, even when there is no clear reason for low self-esteem.

4. Emotional Memory of Past Rejection

People with RSD tend to hold onto emotional pain from past experiences of rejection or failure. These memories can linger, affecting their present-day sense of self-worth.

- **Impact on self-esteem**: When past rejections are mentally replayed or remembered vividly, they reinforce feelings of inadequacy, even if current circumstances are positive. This creates a distorted view of oneself, making it hard to maintain steady self-esteem.

5. Feeling Different or Defective

Individuals with ADHD and RSD may struggle with feeling "different" or out of place, which is amplified by their intense emotional reactions. They may feel that they're somehow flawed for reacting so strongly to situations that others handle with ease.

- **Impact on self-esteem**: This sense of being fundamentally different or defective can lower self-esteem, even if the person doesn't have clear, external reasons for feeling that way. It's an internalized belief that something is inherently wrong with them, even if others don't see it.

6. Negative Internal Dialogue

RSD can fuel a negative inner dialogue where the person constantly doubts their worth or questions their abilities. This internal dialogue is often self-critical and harsh, with little room for positive reinforcement.

- **Impact on self-esteem**: This inner narrative is powerful because it shapes how someone views themselves. If the dominant voice is one of self-criticism, it's hard to build or maintain a positive self-image, even if there are no immediate reasons to feel inadequate.

7. Self-Isolation and Withdrawal

- To avoid the pain of rejection, people with RSD might withdraw from social situations, relationships, or opportunities. This isolation can further contribute to feelings of inadequacy and loneliness.

- **Impact on self-esteem**: Social withdrawal deprives individuals of the positive experiences and feedback that could help build their self-esteem. The isolation reinforces the belief that they are unworthy of connection or success, further lowering self-esteem.

8. Hyperfocus on Perceived Flaws

RSD can cause someone to hyperfocus on their own perceived flaws or mistakes. This means that any minor error can feel like a monumental failure, consuming their thoughts and fueling self-doubt.

- **Impact on self-esteem**: By focusing on perceived failures rather than successes, a person is constantly reinforcing their negative self-perception. This makes it difficult to see their strengths or achievements, which are essential for maintaining healthy self-esteem.

9. Difficulty Accepting Compliments

Because RSD causes someone to be hyperaware of rejection, they might struggle to accept positive feedback or compliments. They may dismiss kind words or interpret them as insincere.

- **Impact on self-esteem**: When positive reinforcement is rejected or dismissed, it becomes harder to internalize positive self-beliefs. Over time, this lack of acceptance of compliments and praise prevents self-esteem from growing.

10. Constant Overcompensation

People with RSD often overcompensate in various areas of life, whether it's at work, in relationships, or with personal achievements. They might push themselves to extremes to avoid any possibility of failure or rejection.

- **Impact on self-esteem**: Overcompensation can lead to burnout, frustration, and feelings of inadequacy when the efforts don't result in perfect outcomes. The constant striving for validation prevents them from feeling "good enough," regardless of how much they accomplish.

RSD creates a complex emotional environment where feelings of rejection and failure are magnified, regardless of external evidence. This makes self-esteem fragile, easily eroded by minor or even imagined slights. Even when there aren't clear reasons for low self-esteem, the intense emotional reactions triggered by RSD are enough to create persistent self-doubt.

Building self-awareness and self-acceptance, learning coping strategies for RSD, and practicing self-compassion can all help individuals manage these emotional challenges, leading to a more stable and positive sense of self-worth.

YOU ARE WIRED DIFFERENTLY

Yes, the fact that people with ADHD and Rejection Sensitive Dysphoria (RSD) are wired to experience heightened emotional sensitivity does indeed make it more challenging to change how they perceive themselves in relation to the world. Here are several reasons why it is difficult, as well as potential ways to approach this challenge:

1. Neurological Wiring and Emotional Sensitivity

ADHD brains are wired to process emotions more intensely, which means that even small criticisms or perceived rejections can feel overwhelming. With RSD, this sensitivity is magnified, causing emotional pain to feel more acute. This hardwiring makes it difficult to rationalize or brush off perceived slights, as the emotional response happens quickly and automatically.

- **Challenge**: Since this heightened sensitivity is part of the neurobiology of ADHD, individuals can feel that their emotional responses are uncontrollable and that they are always at the mercy of how others perceive them. This creates a deeply ingrained belief that they are constantly being judged or rejected.
- **Solution**: While the wiring can't be entirely changed, individuals can learn to *manage* their responses. Strategies like **mindfulness, cognitive behavioral therapy (CBT)**, and **emotional regulation techniques** can help slow down emotional reactions and create space for more rational thinking before feelings of rejection take over.

2. Hyperfocus on Negative Feedback

People with RSD often fixate on negative feedback or perceived rejections, while ignoring or downplaying positive reinforcement. The ADHD brain's tendency to hyperfocus can make them dwell excessively on these negative experiences, reinforcing the idea that they are being viewed negatively by others.

- **Challenge**: The tendency to ruminate on rejection and criticism makes it hard to move past these experiences. It creates a feedback loop where negative thoughts feed into more negative emotions, reinforcing the idea that others always perceive them poorly.
- **Solution**: **Shifting focus** from the negative to the positive is essential, but difficult for people with RSD. A practical strategy is to **actively record positive feedback** or moments of success (like keeping a journal of compliments or achievements) to counterbalance the brain's fixation on the negative. **Externalizing** positive reinforcement can help combat the overwhelming focus on perceived failure.

3. Emotional Memory and Past Experiences

People with RSD are often haunted by vivid emotional memories of past rejections or failures. This emotional memory system reinforces the belief that the world will always reject or criticize them. Each new rejection feels like proof that they are unworthy or flawed.

- **Challenge**: These emotionally charged memories can be difficult to shake off because they reinforce low self-worth over time. When new situations arise, the brain automatically refers back to these past experiences, leading to the assumption that others will always perceive them negatively.

- **Solution: Therapeutic techniques** like **exposure therapy** or **EMDR (Eye Movement Desensitization and Reprocessing)** can help individuals process past rejections in a healthier way. Gradually confronting and re-evaluating these experiences can help reduce their emotional charge and break the association between past rejection and current self-perception.

4. Overemphasis on External Validation

Because RSD makes individuals highly sensitive to how others perceive them, they often rely heavily on external validation to feel secure. This over-reliance can make self-esteem extremely fragile because it depends on how others react in the moment.

- **Challenge**: Relying on others for validation is unstable, especially since perceptions and feedback from others are often beyond one's control. When validation is not received, it reinforces the idea that they are not good enough, deepening the belief that the world sees them negatively.

- **Solution**: **Building internal validation** is key. Practices like **self-compassion** and **self-affirmation** can help shift the focus from needing approval from others to finding a sense of worth from within. It takes time and conscious effort, but recognizing small personal victories and learning to appreciate one's own strengths can help break the cycle of dependence on external validation.

5. Fear of Rejection and Avoidance

Due to the fear of rejection, people with RSD often avoid situations where they could potentially be judged, criticized, or rejected. While this avoids short-term pain, it prevents personal growth and reinforces the belief that they are unworthy or incapable, as they never get the chance to prove otherwise to themselves.

- **Challenge**: Avoidance can lead to isolation, fewer opportunities for success, and lower confidence. It also makes the fear of rejection grow stronger, as the person never experiences positive outcomes that could counteract their fears.
- **Solution**: Facing this fear head-on, often through **gradual exposure** to challenging situations, is one way to start overcoming it. Slowly engaging in situations where rejection might occur, while practicing emotional regulation techniques, can help reduce the intensity of RSD reactions. Over time, positive experiences in these situations can help reshape how the individual perceives themselves in relation to others.

6. Inflexible Beliefs About Self-Perception

RSD can cause individuals to develop rigid beliefs about how they are perceived, often assuming that others see them in a consistently negative light. This rigidity makes it difficult to accept alternate perspectives or more positive interpretations of others' actions.

- **Challenge**: Once these beliefs take hold, they become hard to shift. The brain seeks out evidence that confirms these negative self-perceptions, which makes them self-fulfilling. Even when positive feedback is received, it's often dismissed or downplayed.

- **Solution: Cognitive restructuring** techniques, often used in **Cognitive Behavioral Therapy (CBT),** can help challenge and reframe these inflexible beliefs. By identifying and questioning automatic negative thoughts, individuals can start to open up to the possibility that their assumptions about how others perceive them might be inaccurate or exaggerated.

The Path Forward

While the neurological wiring of ADHD and RSD makes it difficult to change how someone perceives the world, it is not impossible. The emotional intensity and sensitivity are deeply rooted in brain chemistry, but with the right tools and strategies, individuals can gradually shift how they interpret others' reactions and, more importantly, how they perceive themselves. The key lies in **building emotional resilience**, **developing self-awareness**, and **practicing self-acceptance**—understanding that while emotional sensitivity may always be part of their makeup, it doesn't have to define their self-worth.

In summary, changing how someone with ADHD and RSD perceives the world is challenging but achievable through a combination of therapy, mindfulness, emotional regulation, and self-compassion. Though they are wired to be sensitive to rejection, they can learn to manage their responses and build a more positive, stable sense of self over time.

AFFIRMATIONS ARE POWERFUL TOOL

For someone with ADHD and Rejection Sensitive Dysphoria (RSD), affirmations can be a powerful tool to navigate the emotional turbulence of an RSD episode. These affirmations help to ground and reassure them before, during, and after the episode. Here are 10 different affirmations to use in each stage:

Before an RSD Episode

These affirmations are meant to build emotional resilience and prepare for any potential triggers:

1. **"I am worthy of love and respect, no matter what happens today."**
   - This affirms your inherent value, independent of external opinions or criticism.

1. **"I am allowed to feel sensitive, but I will not let it define my worth."**
   - Acknowledging sensitivity as a part of who you are, but it doesn't determine how valuable you are.
1. **"I can't control how others act, but I can control how I respond."**
   - Reminds you of the power you have over your own reactions.
1. **"I am capable of handling difficult emotions, and they will pass."**
   - Prepares you mentally to weather any emotional storms that may come.
1. **"I've overcome tough feelings before, and I will do it again."**
   - Reinforces your ability to manage emotions by drawing on past experiences of resilience.

During an RSD Episode

These affirmations are designed to calm the intense emotions and ground you during the height of the episode:

1. **"This feeling is temporary, and it will pass."**

- Helps you remember that the intensity of the emotions will subside.

1. **"I am more than this moment of pain."**
   - A reminder that you are not defined by this single emotional experience.

1. **"I am loved, and one moment of rejection does not take that away."**
   - Even if you feel rejected, it doesn't negate the love and support you have from others.

1. **"I am safe, even if it feels like I'm being judged."**
   - Acknowledges the feeling of being judged but counters it with a reminder of your emotional and physical safety.

1. **"I am not a failure. This is just a moment, not a reflection of who I am."**
   - Keeps you from internalizing the rejection as a permanent or defining trait.

After an RSD Episode

Once the emotional intensity fades, these affirmations help rebuild your sense of self and prevent lingering feelings of self-doubt or shame:

1. **"I did my best, and that's enough."**

- Affirming that your effort, regardless of the outcome, is enough.

1. **"I am proud of myself for how I handled my emotions."**
   - Validates the way you managed the difficult experience, reinforcing positive emotional regulation.

1. **"I don't need everyone's approval to know I'm worthy."**
   - Helps break the cycle of seeking validation from others to affirm your self-worth.

1. **"I am growing stronger with each emotional challenge I face."**
   - Views the RSD episode as an opportunity for growth, rather than something to fear or regret.

1. **"I deserve kindness and forgiveness, especially from myself."**
   - Encourages self-compassion after an episode, reducing any self-blame or guilt.

These affirmations can help someone with ADHD and RSD navigate the intense emotional landscape before, during, and after an episode. Consistent use of these affirmations can build emotional resilience and cultivate a more positive sense of self, even in the face of overwhelming emotional experiences.

Affirmations can be a powerful tool for individuals who experience severe Rejection Sensitive Dysphoria (RSD) because they help shift thought patterns and emotional responses in moments of distress. For people with RSD, the emotional intensity of perceived rejection or criticism can be overwhelming, often leading to feelings of worthlessness, shame, or emotional pain. Affirmations offer a way to interrupt the emotional spiral and promote healthier self-perception and emotional resilience.

Here's how affirmations can help someone experiencing severe RSD:

1. Interrupting Negative Thought Loops

RSD episodes are often fueled by automatic negative thoughts (ANTs), where a person quickly jumps to conclusions about how others perceive them. Affirmations serve as a mental reset, helping to challenge and reframe those thoughts before they spiral out of control.

- **Example**: Instead of thinking, "They don't like me, I'm a failure," an affirmation like **"I am worthy of respect, regardless of how others respond to me"** can introduce a more balanced perspective and halt the downward emotional spiral.

2. Building Emotional Resilience

Over time, consistent use of affirmations can build emotional resilience by creating new mental pathways. For people with severe RSD, this means they can gradually train their brain to respond less intensely to perceived rejection.

- **Example**: Repeatedly saying **"This feeling is temporary, and I can handle it"** can help someone build the mental toughness needed to navigate intense emotional waves without feeling overwhelmed.

3. Shifting Focus from External to Internal Validation

People with RSD often depend on others for validation, and when they feel rejected or criticized, their self-esteem takes a major hit. Affirmations help shift the focus away from relying on external approval toward internal self-acceptance.

- **Example**: The affirmation **"My worth is not defined by how others treat me"** emphasizes self-validation, reminding the individual that their value is inherent and not dictated by others' actions or opinions.

4. Rewiring Negative Beliefs

Over time, people with RSD may internalize negative beliefs about themselves based on repeated feelings of rejection. Affirmations can help rewrite these beliefs by encouraging more positive and realistic self-perceptions.

- **Example**: If someone constantly feels like they are not good enough, affirmations like **"I am enough as I am, and I deserve kindness"** can slowly replace those ingrained negative beliefs with more supportive ones.

5. Providing Emotional Grounding

During an RSD episode, the emotional intensity can feel overwhelming, causing a person to lose touch with reality and focus solely on the rejection. Affirmations serve as grounding tools, helping individuals reconnect with reality and put their emotions in perspective.

- **Example**: **"This is just a feeling, not a fact"** reminds the person that emotions are transient and do not necessarily reflect the truth of the situation, helping them stay grounded during a storm of emotions.

6. Promoting Self-Compassion

RSD can lead to self-blame and shame, where individuals criticize themselves harshly for feeling sensitive or for how they handled a perceived rejection. Affirmations that encourage self-compassion can counteract these feelings of guilt and shame.

- **Example**: Saying **"I am doing my best, and that's enough"** helps foster self-kindness, allowing the person to accept that they are human and that it's okay to struggle with emotions.

7. Strengthening Emotional Regulation

Affirmations can help individuals develop better emotional regulation skills. By repeating positive and calming phrases, a person can slow down their emotional response and prevent an RSD episode from escalating into a full-blown emotional crisis.

- **Example**: During the onset of an RSD episode, using an affirmation like **"I am in control of how I respond to this situation"** can remind them to take a step back, breathe, and respond more calmly.

8. Increasing Self-Awareness

Affirmations encourage individuals to reflect on their emotions and behaviors in a more constructive way. Instead of reacting impulsively to perceived rejection, affirmations give people a moment to pause and assess whether the rejection is real or imagined, helping them to become more self-aware.

- **Example**: **"I can pause and choose how I react"** reinforces the idea that they have the power to control their emotional responses, increasing self-awareness in the process.

9. Reducing Sensitivity to Criticism

Over time, consistent use of affirmations can reduce an individual's sensitivity to criticism by building confidence and reinforcing a sense of self-worth. As a result, criticisms or perceived rejections won't hit as hard or trigger intense emotional responses as frequently.

- **Example**: Affirming **"I am strong enough to handle criticism without letting it define me"** can help someone with severe RSD become less vulnerable to external judgment.

10. Fostering Long-Term Self-Acceptance

Perhaps the most powerful effect of affirmations is their ability to cultivate long-term self-acceptance. People with RSD often struggle with feeling "flawed" because of their emotional sensitivity, but affirmations can help them embrace who they are, including their emotional intensity.

- **Example**: **"I accept myself fully, even with my sensitivity"** helps the individual come to terms with their emotional responses without viewing them as weaknesses, fostering a deeper sense of self-acceptance.

Writing in a journal can be an incredibly helpful tool for individuals with ADHD and Rejection Sensitive Dysphoria (RSD). Journaling provides a safe space to process emotions, reflect on experiences, and identify thought patterns that contribute to RSD episodes. By journaling, individuals can increase self-awareness, regulate intense emotions, and gain insights into their emotional triggers. It's also a way to practice self-compassion and develop coping strategies over time.

Here are 25 reflective questions that can guide someone with ADHD and RSD in their journaling practice:

Self-Reflection Questions for Emotional Awareness

1. **What triggered my emotional reaction today?**
   - Helps identify specific triggers to become more aware of patterns.
1. **Am I reacting to what happened, or am I reacting to what I think someone thinks of me?**
   - Encourages differentiating between real and perceived rejection.
1. **What did I assume about the situation, and are those assumptions true?**
   - Promotes critical thinking and questions negative thought patterns.
1. **How would I advise a friend in the same situation?**
   - Encourages self-compassion by imagining the advice you'd give to others.
1. **Is this feeling rooted in the past or present?**

- Helps differentiate between unresolved past emotions and current experiences.

1. **How did my body physically react during the emotional episode?**
   - Increases awareness of how emotions manifest physically.

1. **What would it look like if I responded with patience and kindness toward myself?**
   - Encourages gentler self-talk and self-compassion.

1. **How intense was my emotional reaction on a scale of 1 to 10?**
   - Tracks the intensity of emotions and helps identify patterns in severity.

1. **What were my automatic thoughts when I felt rejected?**
   - Allows for identifying and challenging automatic negative thoughts.

1. **What evidence do I have that supports or contradicts my feelings of rejection?**
   - Encourages logical reasoning and fact-checking emotional responses.

Questions for Building Self-Compassion

1. **What are some things I'm proud of about myself today?**
   - Shifts focus to positive achievements and self-worth.
1. **In what ways can I practice kindness toward myself right now?**
   - Encourages immediate acts of self-care and self-kindness.
1. **What do I need to forgive myself for today?**
   - Promotes emotional healing by addressing feelings of guilt or shame.
1. **What strengths helped me get through a difficult moment recently?**
   - Builds awareness of personal strengths in handling challenges.
1. **How can I remind myself that my worth doesn't depend on external validation?**
   - Reinforces internal self-worth rather than relying on others' opinions.
1. **How do I typically speak to myself when I feel rejected, and how can I change that?**
   - Helps identify negative self-talk and creates opportunities for improvement.

1. **What would my inner child need to hear right now to feel safe and loved?**
   - Encourages nurturing self-compassion and care for one's emotional well-being.
1. **What small, positive action can I take today to show myself love?**
   - Promotes practical self-care as a means to restore self-worth.
1. **When have I been resilient in the face of rejection or emotional pain?**
   - Focuses on past resilience to remind oneself of strength and perseverance.
1. **What positive qualities do I possess that I can remind myself of when I feel down?**
   - Reinforces self-affirming thoughts and qualities that build self-esteem.

Questions for Emotional Growth and Self-Acceptance

1. **What did I learn about myself through this difficult experience?**
   - Encourages growth by reflecting on lessons learned from emotional challenges.

1. **What do I wish I had done differently during an RSD episode, and how can I practice that next time?**
   - Helps identify emotional regulation strategies for future experiences.
1. **How do my ADHD traits impact my emotional sensitivity, and how can I work with them instead of against them?**
   - Encourages understanding and acceptance of ADHD traits as part of the process.
1. **How can I reframe this situation to see it as a learning opportunity rather than a setback?**
   - Shifts focus from failure to growth, promoting a positive mindset.
1. **What boundaries can I set to protect my emotional well-being in the future?**
   - Encourages the development of healthy boundaries to reduce future emotional triggers.

How Journaling Helps with RSD:

- **Processing Emotional Intensity:** Writing about emotional experiences allows individuals to put feelings into words, giving structure to emotions that might otherwise feel overwhelming.

- **Tracking Patterns:** Journaling regularly can help identify patterns in emotional responses, triggers, and thought processes, allowing for more intentional self-regulation.

- **Encouraging Self-Compassion:** Reflecting on self-compassion questions can foster kindness toward oneself, reducing the harsh self-criticism often associated with RSD.

- **Promoting Self-Awareness:** Asking reflective questions helps build self-awareness, which is crucial for managing RSD. By understanding how RSD affects emotional responses, individuals can better control their reactions.

- **Building Resilience:** Regular journaling reinforces emotional resilience by acknowledging strengths and past successes, which strengthens one's ability to cope with future emotional difficulties.

By using these questions, someone with ADHD and RSD can cultivate a deeper understanding of their emotional landscape and create a stronger foundation of self-awareness and self-acceptance. This leads to more balanced emotional responses and healthier ways of coping with rejection or criticism.

ADHD & RSD Personality Assessment

Instructions: Reflect on each question and answer as honestly as possible. There are no right or wrong answers. This assessment is designed to help you gain insight into your personality traits related to ADHD and RSD, and how they impact your daily life and emotional well-being. The results from a personality assessment designed for individuals with ADHD and Rejection Sensitive Dysphoria (RSD) can be incredibly valuable for gaining insight into how these traits influence daily life and emotional well-being. Here's a breakdown of how these results can help:

**1. Identifying Key Personality Traits:

The assessment can highlight specific personality traits related to ADHD and RSD, such as heightened sensitivity to criticism, impulsivity, or difficulty with emotional regulation. By understanding these traits, individuals can better comprehend how their ADHD and RSD manifest in their behavior and interactions.

**2. Understanding Emotional Responses:

The assessment can provide insight into how these personality traits affect emotional responses. For example, if the results indicate a high sensitivity to rejection or criticism, individuals can recognize why they might experience intense emotional reactions or RSD episodes in certain situations.

**3. Recognizing Patterns and Triggers:

By analyzing the assessment results, individuals can identify patterns in their emotional responses and behaviors. For instance, they may discover that specific types of feedback or social interactions are more likely to trigger RSD. This awareness can help them anticipate and manage these triggers more effectively.

**4. Developing Targeted Coping Strategies:

The assessment results can guide the development of tailored coping strategies. For example, if the assessment shows a tendency towards impulsivity or emotional reactivity, individuals can focus on strategies that address these specific challenges, such as mindfulness techniques or structured routines.

**5. Enhancing Self-Awareness:

The results offer a deeper understanding of oneself, including strengths and areas for growth. This self-awareness can lead to increased self-acceptance and the ability to work on personal development areas that may be impacting emotional well-being and daily functioning.

6. Improving Communication and Relationships:

Understanding the impact of personality traits on interactions can improve communication and relationships. For example, if the assessment reveals a tendency to misinterpret feedback due to RSD, individuals can work on clarifying communication with others and expressing their needs more effectively.

7. Guiding Therapeutic Goals:

For those working with a therapist, the assessment results can help set specific therapeutic goals. The insights gained can inform the focus of therapy sessions, helping individuals and therapists address the most relevant issues related to ADHD and RSD.

8. Promoting Emotional Regulation:

The assessment can shed light on how certain personality traits affect emotional regulation. By understanding these dynamics, individuals can implement strategies to manage their emotions more effectively, such as practicing relaxation techniques or developing resilience-building habits.

9. Facilitating Personal Growth:

The results can highlight areas for personal growth and development. By recognizing specific challenges and strengths, individuals can create a personalized action plan to work on improving aspects of their personality that impact their daily life and emotional well-being.

10. Enhancing Self-Esteem:

Understanding the nature of their traits and how they impact their emotions can lead to greater self-compassion and improved self-esteem. Recognizing that certain challenges are related to ADHD and RSD, rather than personal failings, can help individuals build a more positive self-image.

11. Providing Insight for Support Systems:

The assessment results can be shared with support systems, such as family members or close friends, to foster understanding and empathy. This can lead to more supportive interactions and accommodations that address specific challenges related to ADHD and RSD.

12. **Tracking Progress:

Repeated assessments can be used to track progress over time. By periodically reviewing results, individuals can monitor changes in their self-awareness, emotional regulation, and coping strategies, adjusting their approach as needed.

13. **Building a Personalized Self-Care Plan:

The assessment can inform the development of a personalized self-care plan. By understanding the unique traits and challenges revealed in the results, individuals can tailor their self-care practices to better address their needs and improve overall well-being.

14. **Enhancing Daily Functioning:

Insights from the assessment can help individuals identify and address specific areas that impact their daily functioning, such as time management, organization, and stress management. By targeting these areas, they can improve their overall efficiency and quality of life.

15. **Fostering a Growth Mindset:

Finally, the assessment encourages a growth mindset by highlighting that personality traits and challenges can be understood and managed over time. This perspective promotes ongoing self-improvement and resilience in the face of ADHD and RSD-related difficulties.

In summary, the results from an ADHD and RSD personality assessment offer valuable insights into how specific traits affect daily life and emotional well-being. By understanding these dynamics, individuals can develop targeted strategies for coping, communication, and personal growth, ultimately leading to improved emotional regulation and overall quality of life.

Section 1: Understanding Your ADHD Traits

1. **How do you typically manage tasks and deadlines?**
   - A. I use detailed plans and reminders to stay on track.
   - B. I often struggle to remember deadlines and tasks without frequent reminders.

- C. I feel overwhelmed by tasks and often procrastinate.

1. **How do you respond to unexpected changes in your routine?**
   - A. I adapt quickly and find alternative solutions.
   - B. I feel anxious and stressed, needing extra time to adjust.
   - C. I become frustrated and may resist the change.

1. **What is your approach to organizing physical spaces (e.g., desk, home)?**
   - A. I keep everything organized with clear systems in place.
   - B. I try to stay organized but often find clutter accumulating.
   - C. I struggle with organization and frequently lose items.

1. **How do you handle long-term projects or goals?**
   - A. I break them down into smaller tasks and work on them steadily.
   - B. I start with enthusiasm but often lose focus over time.
   - C. I find it challenging to stay motivated and may abandon the project.

1. **How do you perceive your ability to concentrate on tasks?**
   - A. I can focus deeply when interested in the task.
   - B. I find it hard to maintain focus, especially on less engaging tasks.
   - C. I struggle with focus consistently, regardless of the task.

Section 2: Exploring Your Rejection Sensitivity

1. **How do you feel when receiving constructive criticism?**
   - A. I view it as an opportunity for growth and improvement.
   - B. I feel hurt initially but try to use it to better myself.
   - C. I become deeply upset and may question my self-worth.

1. **When you perceive rejection or criticism, how does it impact you emotionally?**
   - A. I feel temporarily upset but quickly move past it.
   - B. I feel distressed and may ruminate on the experience.

- C. I experience intense emotional pain and it affects my self-esteem significantly.

1. **How do you typically react to perceived social rejection (e.g., being left out)?**
   - A. I try to understand the situation and move on.
   - B. I feel disappointed and seek reassurance from others.
   - C. I experience severe distress and may withdraw or react defensively.

1. **How does your sensitivity to rejection affect your interactions with others?**
   - A. I communicate openly and address issues as they arise.
   - B. I sometimes hold back to avoid potential rejection or conflict.
   - C. I frequently avoid social interactions to prevent the risk of rejection.

1. **How do you cope with feelings of inadequacy or failure?**
   - A. I acknowledge the feelings but remind myself of my strengths and achievements.
   - B. I feel discouraged and may seek support from friends or professionals.

- C. I struggle to overcome these feelings and may experience prolonged self-doubt.

Section 3: Self-Awareness and Coping Strategies

1. **What strategies do you use to manage your emotions during stressful situations?**
   - A. I use relaxation techniques and positive self-talk.
   - B. I try to distract myself or seek support from others.
   - C. I often feel overwhelmed and have difficulty managing my emotions.

1. **How do you prioritize self-care and personal well-being in your daily life?**
   - A. I make self-care a regular part of my routine and set aside time for myself.
   - B. I try to incorporate self-care but often neglect it due to other demands.
   - C. I struggle to find time for self-care and often put others' needs first.

1. **How do you approach problem-solving when faced with a challenge?**
   - A. I analyze the situation and explore multiple solutions.

- o B. I try to solve problems but can become frustrated if solutions aren't clear.
- o C. I feel overwhelmed by challenges and may avoid addressing them.

1. **What role does self-compassion play in how you deal with setbacks or mistakes?**
   - o A. I practice self-compassion and treat myself with kindness.
   - o B. I try to be compassionate but often struggle with self-criticism.
   - o C. I find it hard to be kind to myself and may be very self-critical.

1. **How do you perceive your progress in personal growth and self-improvement?**
   - o A. I recognize my progress and celebrate small achievements.
   - o B. I acknowledge some progress but often focus on areas needing improvement.
   - o C. I feel like I'm not making significant progress and may become discouraged.

Scoring and Interpretation

To interpret your responses:

- **Mostly A's:** You have a strong sense of self-awareness and effective strategies for managing ADHD and RSD. You use constructive approaches to handle challenges and emotional responses.
- **Mostly B's:** You are aware of your traits and challenges but may need to refine your strategies for managing ADHD and RSD. You might benefit from additional coping mechanisms and self-care practices.
- **Mostly C's:** You may struggle significantly with ADHD and RSD-related challenges. Consider seeking professional support to develop more effective coping strategies and enhance self-awareness.

Next Steps

1. **Reflect on Your Results:** Use the insights gained from this assessment to identify areas where you might need support or development.
2. **Set Goals:** Establish specific goals to address areas of challenge, such as improving organization skills, developing self-compassion, or managing emotional reactions.
3. **Seek Support:** Consider working with a mental health professional who specializes in ADHD and RSD to

develop personalized strategies for managing your symptoms.

4. **Implement Coping Strategies:** Incorporate practical coping strategies into your daily routine to address the challenges identified in the assessment.

By understanding your traits and how they influence your experiences, you can take proactive steps to manage ADHD and RSD more effectively and enhance your overall well-being.

Cognitive Behavioral Therapy (CBT) is a

therapeutic approach that helps individuals identify and challenge negative thought patterns and behaviors and replace them with healthier alternatives. Here are five different CBT exercises that can be useful for managing ADHD and Rejection Sensitive Dysphoria (RSD):

1. Cognitive Restructuring

Objective: To identify and challenge negative thought patterns.

Steps:

1. **Identify a Negative Thought:**

- Write down a specific negative thought you experienced. For example, "I always mess things up."

1. **Evaluate the Evidence:**
   - List evidence that supports and contradicts this thought. For example, evidence supporting it might include past mistakes, while evidence against it might include successes or instances where you managed tasks well.

1. **Challenge the Thought:**
   - Ask yourself: "Is this thought accurate?" "Are there other ways to view this situation?"

1. **Replace with a Balanced Thought:**
   - Create a more balanced or positive thought based on the evidence. For example, "I make mistakes sometimes, but I also have many successes. I can learn from my mistakes and improve."

1. **Reflect on the New Thought:**
   - Write down how this new, balanced thought makes you feel compared to the original negative thought.

2. Thought Record

Objective: To track and analyze thoughts and their impact on emotions and behaviors.

Steps:

1. **Record the Situation:**
   - Write down a specific situation that triggered a negative thought or emotion. For example, "I received feedback on my work."

1. **Describe the Thought:**
   - Record the exact thought you had in response to the situation. For example, "I'm a failure because I got criticism."

1. **Identify the Emotion:**
   - Note the emotions you felt and rate their intensity from 1 to 10. For example, "Feeling anxious, 8/10."

1. **Evaluate the Thought:**
   - Analyze the accuracy of the thought. Ask yourself: "Is this thought based on facts or assumptions?" "What evidence do I have?"

1. **Develop an Alternative Thought:**
   - Create a more balanced or positive thought. For example, "Criticism is an opportunity for growth, and I can improve my skills."

1. **Reflect on the Change:**

o   Record how your emotions and beliefs changed after adopting the new thought.

3. Behavioral Experiments

Objective: To test the validity of negative beliefs through experimentation.

Steps:

1. **Identify a Negative Belief:**
   o   Write down a negative belief you hold. For example, "If I speak up in meetings, people will think I'm annoying."

1. **Design an Experiment:**
   o   Plan a small, manageable action to test this belief. For example, speak up in a meeting and share a brief idea.

1. **Predict the Outcome:**
   o   Predict what will happen and how you'll feel. For example, "I'll be judged negatively and feel embarrassed."

1. **Conduct the Experiment:**
   o   Carry out the action and observe the outcome. Note the actual results and compare them with your predictions.

1. **Reflect on the Results:**
   - Analyze what happened. Was your prediction accurate? What did you learn from this experience? Adjust your belief based on the new evidence.

4. Activity Scheduling and Planning

Objective: To manage tasks and reduce procrastination by planning activities.

Steps:

1. **List Tasks:**
   - Write down all the tasks or activities you need to complete. Include both work-related and personal tasks.
1. **Prioritize and Break Down:**
   - Prioritize tasks based on importance and urgency. Break larger tasks into smaller, manageable steps.
1. **Create a Schedule:**
   - Use a planner or calendar to schedule specific times for each task. Include breaks and leisure activities to avoid burnout.
1. **Monitor Your Progress:**

- As you complete tasks, check them off your list. Reflect on what worked well and what could be improved.

1. **Adjust as Needed:**
   - If you find certain tasks are consistently not being completed, adjust your approach. This might involve re-prioritizing or breaking tasks down further.

5. Mindfulness and Grounding Techniques

Objective: To manage overwhelming emotions and stay present.

Steps:

1. **Choose a Mindfulness Exercise:**
   - Select a mindfulness exercise, such as deep breathing, progressive muscle relaxation, or a body scan.

1. **Set Aside Time:**
   - Allocate a specific time each day to practice mindfulness. Start with 5-10 minutes.

1. **Focus on the Present Moment:**
   - Engage in the mindfulness exercise, focusing on your breath, physical sensations, or surroundings.

If your mind wanders, gently bring it back to the present moment.

1. **Reflect on the Experience:**
   - After the exercise, reflect on how you feel. Note any changes in your emotional state or stress levels.

1. **Integrate Mindfulness into Daily Life:**
   - Look for opportunities to practice mindfulness throughout your day, such as during routine activities or moments of stress.

How These Exercises Help:

1. **Cognitive Restructuring** and **Thought Records** help challenge and change negative thinking patterns, reducing the impact of RSD.
2. **Behavioral Experiments** test the validity of negative beliefs and provide real-world evidence to challenge those beliefs.
3. **Activity Scheduling and Planning** help manage tasks and reduce procrastination, which can alleviate stress and improve overall functioning.
4. **Mindfulness and Grounding Techniques** help manage overwhelming emotions and stay grounded, reducing the intensity of RSD episodes.

Incorporating these CBT exercises into your routine can enhance self-awareness, improve emotional regulation, and help manage the impact of ADHD and RSD on your daily life.

Self-Awareness Assessment for ADHD and RSD

Questions:

50 thoughtful questions that can be used in a **Self-Awareness Assessment** for individuals with ADHD and **Rejection Sensitive Dysphoria (RSD)**. These questions focus on various aspects such as emotional regulation, core beliefs, triggers, behaviors, and interpersonal relationships.

Instructions: Answer each question based on your personal experiences. Use the following scale for your responses:

1. General Self-Awareness
2. How often do you feel overwhelmed by your emotions?

3. Do you find it challenging to understand why you're feeling a certain way?

4. How well do you feel you know your personal strengths and weaknesses?

5. What are your typical responses when someone criticizes you, even if it's constructive?

6. How often do you feel like you're not meeting your own expectations?

7. When things don't go as planned, how do you usually react?

8. Do you tend to replay past mistakes or failures in your mind? How often?

9. How comfortable are you with asking for help when you need it?

10. Do you frequently compare yourself to others, and how does this make you feel?

11. Do you feel misunderstood by others? If so, in what ways?

12. Emotional Regulation & RSD

13. How do you typically handle rejection or perceived rejection?

14. How long do feelings of rejection or criticism linger for you?

15. Do you ever feel like your emotional reactions are stronger than the situation warrants?
16. When feeling rejected or criticized, what thoughts typically go through your mind?
17. Are you able to calm yourself down when you're upset? If so, how do you do it?
18. How often do you experience emotional breakdowns after small disagreements or criticisms?
19. When rejected, do you feel physical symptoms like a racing heart, sweating, or shaking?
20. What do you tell yourself to feel better after a negative emotional event?
21. How often do you avoid certain situations or people because you fear rejection?
22. Do you experience shame or guilt after reacting emotionally to criticism?

Core Beliefs & Self-Perception

1. What are the most common negative thoughts you have about yourself?
2. How often do you feel like you're not good enough?
3. What core beliefs do you think drive most of your emotional reactions?

4. Do you believe you need to be perfect to be accepted or loved?

5. How often do you feel like you don't deserve the success or happiness you experience?

6. How often do you feel like you're a burden to others?

7. When you succeed, do you tend to credit yourself or dismiss it as luck or someone else's help?

8. Do you think people would like you more if you behaved differently?

9. How much of your self-worth is dependent on other people's opinions of you?

10. Do you often feel like you're different from others in a way that makes you feel isolated?

Triggers & Emotional Patterns

1. What types of situations or comments are most likely to trigger a strong emotional response?

2. Can you recognize when an emotional reaction is due to a core belief being triggered?

3. How often do you feel emotionally triggered in your personal relationships?

4. When you're triggered, do you notice a pattern in how you react?

5. Are you able to anticipate certain situations that may lead to emotional distress?

6. Do you ever feel like small, insignificant comments have a bigger emotional impact than they should?

7. How often do past experiences of rejection influence your current decisions?

8. Are there certain people or places that make you feel more emotionally vulnerable?

9. How aware are you of your emotional triggers and what causes them?

Perfectionism & Black-and-White Thinking

1. Do you tend to think in extremes, such as viewing things as either a success or a failure?

2. How often do you set unrealistic expectations for yourself?

3. Do you feel like any mistake is a reflection of your overall worth or abilities?

4. How much does fear of failure influence the decisions you make?

5. Are you overly focused on doing things perfectly, even if it's unrealistic or unnecessary?

6. When faced with criticism, do you find it difficult to see the situation from a balanced perspective?

7. How do you react when things don't go exactly as planned?

8. Do you often think that if something isn't perfect, it's a total failure?

9. How often do you struggle with procrastination due to fear of not doing something perfectly?

10. Do you ever avoid challenges because you fear they might confirm your worst beliefs about yourself?

11. Do you find it difficult to accept praise or recognition for your efforts, always feeling like you could have done more?

Scoring and Interpretation

To interpret your responses:

- **1** = Not at all true
- **2** = Slightly true
- **3** = Moderately true
- **4** = Very true
- **5** = Extremely true

1. **Total Your Scores:** Add up your scores for all 20 questions.

2. **Determine Your Self-Awareness Level:**

   - **20-40: Low Self-Awareness**

     You may have limited insight into how ADHD and RSD affect your life. Consider exploring these issues further and seeking support to enhance your self-awareness.

   - **41-60: Moderate Self-Awareness**

     You have some understanding of how ADHD and RSD impact your life, but there may be areas for growth. Focus on identifying and addressing any gaps in your self-awareness.

   - **61-80: High Self-Awareness**

     You have a strong sense of how ADHD and RSD affect your life and interactions. You are likely able to recognize patterns and apply strategies to manage these challenges effectively.

   - **81-100: Very High Self-Awareness**

     You exhibit a deep understanding of how ADHD and RSD influence your thoughts, behaviors, and relationships. You likely have effective strategies in place and a clear awareness of how to navigate your experiences.

Next Steps:

- **For Low to Moderate Self-Awareness:** Consider working with a mental health professional to deepen your understanding and develop effective strategies for managing ADHD and RSD.
- **For High to Very High Self-Awareness:** Continue to build on your insights and explore advanced coping strategies and self-care practices. Regular reflection can help maintain and enhance your self-awareness.

This assessment can be a valuable tool in understanding how well you are aware of your ADHD and RSD traits and how they impact your daily life.

Understanding RSD Episodes:

It's important to recognize that once a Rejection Sensitive Dysphoria (RSD) episode begins, it can be extremely difficult to stop. RSD is deeply wired into our brains, making it a challenging condition to control. These episodes are not just reactions but are part of a complex neurological response that doesn't easily relent.

Change and improvement in managing RSD do not happen overnight. The process of learning to manage and mitigate RSD symptoms can take months, years, or, in some cases, may not result in complete change. It's crucial to understand that the nature of RSD makes it a persistent and deeply ingrained aspect of your emotional experience.

While it may be challenging to fully alter these responses, seeking support, developing coping strategies, and practicing self-compassion can help you navigate the difficulties associated with RSD. Acknowledging the persistent nature of RSD and approaching it with patience and persistence is key to managing its impact on your life.

Understanding why Rejection Sensitive Dysphoria (RSD) feels so overwhelming and challenging to control involves delving into the neurobiological and psychological mechanisms underlying this condition. Here's a detailed explanation of how RSD is wired in the brain and why it feels so difficult to manage:

**1. Neurobiological Basis of RSD

RSD is often thought to be linked to how the brain processes and responds to rejection, criticism, or perceived failure. Several key brain areas and neurotransmitter systems are involved:

- **Amygdala:** This part of the brain is crucial for processing emotions, especially fear and anxiety. In individuals with RSD, the amygdala can become highly reactive to perceived threats or negative feedback, leading to intense emotional responses. This heightened activity can make it challenging to regulate emotions and control reactions.
- **Prefrontal Cortex:** The prefrontal cortex is responsible for executive functions such as decision-making, reasoning, and impulse control. In people with RSD, this area may struggle to exert control over the amygdala's emotional responses, leading to a disproportionate emotional reaction to rejection or criticism.
- **Neurotransmitters:** Imbalances in neurotransmitters like serotonin and dopamine, which play roles in mood regulation and reward processing, can influence how we experience and react to rejection. Disruptions in these systems can exacerbate the emotional intensity of RSD.

**2. Why It's Challenging to Stop RSD Episodes

RSD episodes are difficult to control due to several factors:

- **Automatic Response:** RSD responses are often automatic and unconscious. When faced with rejection or criticism, the brain's emotional response can be swift and intense, bypassing logical thought processes. This automatic reaction can make it challenging to pause and apply rational thinking in the moment.

- **Intensity of Emotions:** The emotional intensity experienced during an RSD episode can overwhelm logical thinking. The amygdala's response can flood the brain with distressing emotions, making it hard for the prefrontal cortex to intervene and rationalize the situation.

- **Cognitive Distortions:** RSD can lead to cognitive distortions such as catastrophizing (assuming the worst-case scenario) and personalization (taking things personally). These distortions can reinforce negative emotions and make it harder to see the situation objectively.

**3. Emotional Brain Dominance

The emotional brain often feels like it has taken control due to the following reasons:

- **Emotional Hijacking:** The term "emotional hijacking" describes how intense emotions can override logical thinking. When the amygdala is activated, it can overpower the prefrontal cortex's ability to regulate and process emotions rationally.
- **Evolutionary Perspective:** From an evolutionary standpoint, the brain's emotional responses are designed to protect us from threats. Rejection and criticism can be perceived as social threats, triggering a strong emotional response that prioritizes immediate reaction over thoughtful analysis.
- **Neurological Wiring:** The neural pathways associated with RSD are reinforced over time through repeated experiences of rejection and emotional pain. These pathways become more ingrained, making it harder to change the automatic responses even with cognitive effort.

**4. Challenges in Using Logic

Logic and rational thinking often struggle to gain traction during an RSD episode due to:

- **Emotional Overwhelm:** When emotions are extremely intense, they can cloud judgment and make it difficult to think clearly. The emotional brain's activation can overpower the logical processes, making rational thought seem distant or irrelevant.

- **Perception of Threat:** During an RSD episode, perceived threats (like rejection) are processed with high urgency. This heightened perception of threat can make logical thinking seem secondary or ineffective in addressing the immediate emotional turmoil.

- **Difficulty in Shifting Focus:** Shifting from an emotional response to logical analysis requires cognitive effort. During an RSD episode, this effort can be challenging due to the overwhelming nature of the emotional experience.

**5. Managing and Mitigating RSD

While it may not be possible to completely eliminate RSD, there are strategies to manage and mitigate its impact:

- **Cognitive Behavioral Techniques:** Techniques such as cognitive restructuring can help challenge and reframe negative thoughts associated with RSD.

- **Mindfulness and Emotional Regulation:** Mindfulness practices can help increase awareness of emotional responses and develop skills to regulate them.
- **Therapeutic Support:** Working with a therapist can provide strategies and support for understanding and managing RSD.
- **Self-Compassion:** Practicing self-compassion can help mitigate the effects of rejection and reduce the intensity of emotional reactions.

Understanding that RSD is a complex and deeply ingrained aspect of ADHD can help individuals approach it with patience and compassion. While complete control may not be possible, developing strategies to manage and cope with RSD can lead to improvements in emotional well-being and daily functioning.

Problems Explaining RSD to Someone Else?

For someone who hasn't experienced intense feelings, it might be difficult to fully grasp what a person with ADHD and Rejection Sensitive Dysphoria (RSD) goes through during an emotional breakdown. I'll try to explain it in a way that highlights the depth of the experience, the triggers, and the emotional intensity involved.

What RSD Feels Like for Someone with ADHD

Imagine a scenario where a seemingly small or ordinary situation, such as a mild criticism, a simple mistake, or even a neutral comment, triggers an overwhelming emotional reaction. This is the core of an RSD experience — it is *not* about being overly sensitive in a general sense, but about how the brain of someone with RSD processes perceived rejection or criticism as a deeply personal attack.

Trigger: Perceived Rejection

For someone with RSD, any form of rejection, even slight or imagined, can feel catastrophic. This isn't limited to explicit rejection (e.g., being told "no" or criticized harshly) — it can also be triggered by:

- A disapproving look
- Someone not responding quickly to a text or call
- Mild feedback, like "you could improve this"
- Feeling left out of plans or conversations

For someone without RSD, these situations might be seen as minor inconveniences, but for a person with RSD, they feel like a confirmation of their worst fears — that they are not good enough, unworthy, or unlovable.

The Emotional Breakdown: Intensity Beyond Logic

When the trigger happens, the emotional response is immediate and intense. It's like a tidal wave of emotion hitting all at once, and logic takes a back seat. There's no gradual buildup; instead, it feels like an explosion of distress. Here's what that might feel like for someone with ADHD and RSD:

1. **Overwhelming Sadness or Despair:**
   - The person may feel a crushing sense of sadness, as if they've been rejected or abandoned in a profound way. It feels disproportionate to the trigger, but the intensity is real. For them, it's not just a small criticism — it's proof that they're a failure or unworthy of love or respect.
1. **Shame and Self-Loathing:**
   - Intense feelings of shame flood in. A person with RSD often internalizes rejection, believing that

they are fundamentally flawed. They might start to have thoughts like, "I'm terrible," "I'm always messing things up," or "No one could ever really care about me." This isn't just a fleeting moment of doubt; it feels deeply ingrained.

1. **Panic and Anxiety:**
   - The emotional breakdown often includes panic or anxiety. It's as if their entire sense of self-worth is crumbling. The anxiety comes from trying to figure out what went wrong, why they are being "rejected," and how they can fix it, often leading to obsessive thoughts.

1. **Anger or Irritability:**
   - Sometimes, the emotional response may include anger, directed at themselves or others. The frustration of feeling misunderstood or rejected can boil over, leading to irritability. It's not uncommon for someone with RSD to lash out in an attempt to protect themselves emotionally, only to feel even worse afterward.

Feeling Like Losing Control:

During an RSD episode, the individual often feels completely out of control of their emotions. The part of the brain responsible for logic and reasoning — the prefrontal cortex — seems inaccessible. The amygdala (the brain's emotional center) takes over, and the individual is overwhelmed by their feelings.

For someone observing from the outside, it might seem like the reaction is exaggerated or illogical, but for the person going through it, it feels completely rational. At that moment, they are *convinced* that they are being rejected or criticized in a deep and personal way.

After the Breakdown: Emotional Fallout

Once the intense emotions start to subside, the person might feel exhausted, ashamed, or embarrassed. Often, they recognize that their reaction was disproportionate, but the emotional pain was so real that it was almost impossible to control.

- Exhaustion: After the breakdown, the person often feels drained, both physically and mentally, due to the sheer intensity of the emotional experience.
- Self-Criticism: They may engage in self-criticism, feeling guilty for "overreacting" or for potentially damaging their relationships.

- Lingering Fear: The fear of future rejection might stick around, making them more cautious or anxious in similar situations.

Why Logic Doesn't Help in the Moment:

During an RSD episode, it's extremely difficult for someone to think logically. The emotional brain (amygdala) overrides the logical brain (prefrontal cortex), which is why calm reasoning often doesn't work. A well-meaning friend or family member might say, "It's not that big of a deal" or "You're overreacting," but these statements usually don't help because they don't match the emotional intensity the person is feeling.

In that moment, logic feels irrelevant because the emotional pain is so overwhelming. It's like telling someone who is drowning to just "calm down and swim" — even if they know how to swim, they're still consumed by the immediate panic and fear.

Summing It Up:

For someone with ADHD and RSD, the experience of rejection or criticism triggers an intense, often uncontrollable emotional response. The emotions feel overwhelming, like the brain has been hijacked by feelings of shame, panic, and sadness. Logic is sidelined, and the person feels out of control. It's not something they can simply "snap out of," and the experience often leaves lasting emotional scars.

If you've never felt intense emotions like this, it might be hard to fully relate, but imagine feeling like a deep wound has just been opened every time you experience rejection, no matter how small or unintentional it seems. The emotional response is real and very painful, even though it may not align with the external reality of the situation.

Journal Prompts

Here is a list of **100 ADHD and RSD journal prompts** to help with self-discovery. These prompts are designed to encourage deeper reflection on how ADHD and **Rejection Sensitive Dysphoria (RSD)** affect your emotions, behaviors, relationships, and self-perception.

General Self-Discovery Prompts

1. What is one aspect of your personality that you are most proud of, and why?
2. How does having ADHD affect the way you view yourself compared to others?
3. In what ways do you think your ADHD traits have helped you succeed?
4. Write about a time when you felt different from others. How did that make you feel?
5. How do you define success in your own terms? How does ADHD impact your view of success?
6. What does self-acceptance mean to you, and how does it look in your daily life?
7. Reflect on a recent situation where your ADHD traits either helped or hindered you.
8. How does your ADHD influence your creativity? Give examples.
9. What is the biggest challenge you face when managing your ADHD?
10. Describe a time when you felt overwhelmed by your emotions. What did you do to manage it?

Emotional Regulation & RSD

1. How do you usually feel after receiving criticism? How long does that feeling last?
2. Write about a time when you felt rejected. How did it impact you emotionally?
3. What physical sensations do you experience when you feel emotionally overwhelmed?
4. What are some healthy ways you can self-soothe when feeling rejected or criticized?
5. How often do you feel misunderstood by others? Write about a recent instance.
6. What thoughts tend to run through your mind when someone criticizes you?
7. How do you usually recover from emotional distress? What helps and what doesn't?
8. What does self-compassion look like for you after you experience a rejection?
9. Reflect on a time when someone's words or actions hurt you more than they should have.
10. How does RSD influence the way you approach relationships and friendships?

Core Beliefs & Self-Perception

1. What are three core beliefs you hold about yourself? Are they positive or negative?

2. How has ADHD shaped your beliefs about your abilities and potential?

3. Write about a time when you felt "less than" others due to your ADHD. How did you cope?

4. What are some assumptions you make about yourself when things go wrong?

5. Do you feel like you're not enough? Why or why not? Explore those feelings.

6. Reflect on the differences between your self-perception and how others see you.

7. What core belief tends to get triggered when you face criticism or rejection?

8. How often do you believe you need to be perfect to be valued by others?

9. How do you define your self-worth? Is it tied to other people's opinions or something internal?

10. What positive affirmations can you use to challenge negative core beliefs about yourself?

Triggers & Emotional Patterns

1. What are the most common emotional triggers you face in your everyday life?

2. How do you usually respond to emotional triggers? Is there a pattern to your reactions?

3. Write about a recent emotional trigger. How did it make you feel, and how did you react?

4. How aware are you of the situations or people who trigger your emotions?

5. When you're triggered emotionally, what coping strategies work best for you?

6. How does fear of rejection influence your decisions in social or work situations?

7. What are some things you can do to prevent being triggered by rejection or criticism?

8. How do you feel about making mistakes? What triggers those emotions?

9. Write about a time when an insignificant comment triggered a big emotional response.

10. Reflect on how your triggers are connected to your past experiences of rejection.

Perfectionism & Black-and-White Thinking

1. How does perfectionism show up in your daily life? How does it affect you?

2. Write about a time when you felt like you had to be perfect to be accepted.

3. How do you react when things don't go exactly as planned? Explore those feelings.

4. Do you tend to see things as "all or nothing"? How does this affect your life?

5. Reflect on a recent situation where you thought in black-and-white terms. How could you view it more realistically?

6. How does fear of failure or imperfection hold you back from taking risks?

7. Write about how you can shift from perfectionistic thinking to self-compassion.

8. How often do you avoid challenges because you're afraid of not doing them perfectly?

9. What does "failure" mean to you? How do you cope when you experience it?

10. How does your self-esteem fluctuate depending on whether you succeed or fail?

Self-Compassion & Self-Worth

1. What does self-compassion mean to you, and how can you practice it more often?

2. Write a letter to your past self, offering compassion and understanding for your struggles.

3. How does your ADHD affect your self-esteem? Reflect on its impact.

4. What are some ways you can be kinder to yourself when you feel overwhelmed?

5. How does RSD influence your feelings of self-worth after receiving negative feedback?

6. What small acts of self-care can you incorporate into your routine to build self-worth?

7. Reflect on the connection between self-compassion and emotional resilience.

8. How do you treat yourself after you make a mistake or face rejection? Is it kind or harsh?

9. What can you do to nurture a more positive relationship with yourself?

10. Write about a recent accomplishment, no matter how small. How did it make you feel?

Relationships & Social Interactions

1. How does your fear of rejection affect your relationships with others?

2. Reflect on how ADHD impacts your ability to communicate with friends and family.

3. How do you tend to react when someone misunderstands or misjudges you?

4. Write about a time when you avoided a social situation out of fear of rejection.

5. How comfortable are you in setting boundaries with others? What makes it challenging?
6. What are some ways you can build healthier communication in your relationships?
7. How does criticism from loved ones affect you emotionally, and how do you handle it?
8. Write about a relationship where you feel fully accepted. How does that make you feel?
9. What do you need from others to feel emotionally safe in a relationship?
10. How do you balance your emotional needs with the needs of others in your relationships?

Growth & Resilience

1. How have you grown as a person despite the challenges of ADHD and RSD?
2. What lessons have you learned from past experiences of rejection or failure?
3. Write about a time when you overcame an emotional challenge. What did you learn?
4. How do you practice emotional resilience in the face of criticism or setbacks?
5. Reflect on a moment of personal growth where you turned a negative experience into something positive.

6. How can you challenge negative thoughts and replace them with more empowering ones?

7. What are your top three coping strategies for managing emotional distress?

8. Write about a personal strength that has helped you navigate emotional challenges.

9. How does mindfulness or meditation help you regulate your emotions? If you haven't tried, would you be open to it?

10. What are some new strategies you can try to help you manage emotional triggers better?

Overcoming Fear of Rejection

1. Write about a time when you felt rejected. How can you reframe that experience to see it differently?

2. How does your fear of rejection hold you back from pursuing what you want?

3. What steps can you take to overcome your fear of rejection in social situations?

4. Reflect on how often you say "yes" to things you don't want to do to avoid rejection.

5. How can you practice being more assertive without fearing the response of others?

6. What would your life look like if you didn't fear rejection? Explore the possibilities.

7. Write about a time when you stood up for yourself. How did it feel afterward?

8. How can you challenge the idea that rejection defines your worth?

9. What is one way you can practice resilience after experiencing a rejection?

10. How can you set healthier emotional boundaries in your life to avoid overextending yourself?

Goals & Moving Forward

1. What are three goals you have for improving your emotional regulation? How can you work toward them?

2. Reflect on how your ADHD affects your ability to reach your goals. How can you work with your ADHD instead of against it?

3. What are some habits you'd like to build to strengthen your emotional well-being?

4. How can you turn emotional pain into a learning experience to help you grow?

5. What is one thing you can do today to boost your self-confidence?

6. Write about a time when you thought you failed but later realized you learned something valuable.

7. How can you use past emotional experiences to better prepare yourself for future challenges?

8. Write about a specific goal you have and how you plan to manage the emotional ups and downs along the way.

9. What steps can you take to feel more empowered in situations where you usually feel rejected?

10. Reflect on how far you've come in your self-awareness journey. What are you most proud of?

10 coping strategies specifically designed to help individuals manage Rejection Sensitive Dysphoria (RSD) effectively:

1. Mindfulness Meditation

- **Description**: Practice mindfulness meditation to stay present and grounded. This technique helps you observe your thoughts and emotions without judgment, reducing the intensity of emotional reactions.

- **How to Use**: Set aside a few minutes each day to sit quietly and focus on your breath. When you notice your mind wandering, gently bring your focus back to your breath.

2. Cognitive Restructuring

- **Description**: Use cognitive restructuring to challenge and reframe negative thoughts that arise during RSD episodes. This involves identifying distorted thinking patterns and replacing them with more balanced thoughts.
- **How to Use**: When you experience a negative thought, ask yourself if it's based on facts or assumptions. Then, write down a more balanced thought that reflects reality.

3. Self-Compassion Practices

- **Description**: Engage in self-compassion exercises to treat yourself with kindness and understanding. This approach helps to counteract feelings of shame and self-criticism.

- **How to Use**: Practice self-compassion by writing a letter to yourself as if you were writing to a friend. Offer yourself words of encouragement and support.

4. Emotion Regulation Techniques

- **Description**: Use techniques to manage and regulate intense emotions. This includes deep breathing, progressive muscle relaxation, and grounding exercises.
- **How to Use**: Practice deep breathing by inhaling slowly through your nose, holding for a few seconds, and exhaling through your mouth. Repeat several times until you feel calmer.

5. Journaling

- **Description**: Keep a journal to track your emotional experiences and reflect on RSD episodes. Journaling helps you gain insights into your triggers and responses.
- **How to Use**: Write about your daily experiences, focusing on events that trigger RSD and your emotional reactions. Include reflections on what you learned and how you might handle similar situations in the future.

6. Setting Boundaries

- **Description**: Establish and maintain boundaries to protect your emotional well-being. This can involve setting limits on how much time you spend with certain people or in specific environments.
- **How to Use**: Identify areas where you need to set boundaries to prevent emotional overload. Communicate these boundaries clearly and assertively to others.

7. Seeking Support

- **Description**: Reach out for support from trusted friends, family members, or support groups. Sharing your experiences with others who understand RSD can provide comfort and reduce feelings of isolation.
- **How to Use**: Find a support group or community where you can discuss your experiences with RSD. Share your feelings and listen to others for mutual support.

8. Engaging in Hobbies and Interests

- **Description**: Pursue hobbies and interests that bring you joy and relaxation. Engaging in activities you enjoy can provide a positive outlet for your emotions.

- **How to Use**: Identify activities that you find fulfilling and make time for them regularly. Whether it's painting, gardening, or playing a musical instrument, choose activities that help you unwind.

9. Establishing a Routine

- **Description**: Create and follow a daily routine to bring structure and predictability to your life. A consistent routine can help manage stress and reduce the impact of RSD.
- **How to Use**: Develop a daily schedule that includes time for work, self-care, and relaxation. Stick to your routine as closely as possible to create a sense of stability.

10. Professional Counseling

- **Description**: Seek guidance from a mental health professional who specializes in ADHD and emotional regulation. Professional counseling can provide tailored strategies and support for managing RSD.
- **How to Use**: Find a therapist or counselor with experience in treating ADHD and RSD. Attend regular sessions to work on coping strategies and address underlying issues related to RSD.

Implementing these coping strategies can help individuals manage their RSD more effectively, leading to improved emotional well-being and resilience.

Creating a comprehensive 100-question multiple-choice quiz on ADHD and Rejection Sensitive Dysphoria (RSD) can be a useful tool for assessing knowledge and understanding of these topics. Here is a detailed quiz, followed by the answers:

ADHD and RSD Quiz

Questions

1. **What does RSD stand for?**
   - A) Rejection Sensitive Disorder
   - B) Rejection Sensitivity Dysphoria
   - C) Reactive Sensory Dysphoria
   - D) Rejection Sensitivity Disorder
1. **Which population is most commonly associated with RSD?**
   - A) Individuals with PTSD
   - B) Individuals with ADHD
   - C) Individuals with Bipolar Disorder
   - D) Individuals with Autism Spectrum Disorder
1. **What is a primary symptom of RSD?**

- A) Difficulty focusing
- B) Severe emotional pain from perceived rejection
- C) Impulsive behavior
- D) Hyperactivity

1. **Which of the following is NOT a common trigger for RSD episodes?**
   - A) Criticism
   - B) Rejection
   - C) Success
   - D) Failure

1. **What is the primary emotional response in RSD?**
   - A) Joy
   - B) Indifference
   - C) Intense sadness or anger
   - D) Euphoria

1. **How does RSD affect self-esteem?**
   - A) It improves self-esteem
   - B) It has no effect on self-esteem
   - C) It decreases self-esteem
   - D) It stabilizes self-esteem

1. **Which therapeutic approach is commonly used to help manage RSD?**
   - A) Cognitive Behavioral Therapy (CBT)

- B) Dialectical Behavior Therapy (DBT)
- C) Art Therapy
- D) Music Therapy

1. **What is a common behavioral reaction during an RSD episode?**
   - A) Overachievement
   - B) Isolation
   - C) Enhanced productivity
   - D) Increased social interaction

1. **In which manual is RSD not explicitly recognized?**
   - A) DSM-5
   - B) ICD-10
   - C) DSM-IV
   - D) DSM-V

1. **Which of the following is NOT a characteristic of ADHD?**
   - A) Impulsivity
   - B) Hyperactivity
   - C) Excessive self-doubt
   - D) Inattention

1. **What role does self-awareness play in managing RSD?**
   - A) It has no impact on RSD

- B) It helps in recognizing and addressing emotional responses
- C) It worsens RSD symptoms
- D) It replaces the need for therapy

1. **What is a common outcome of prolonged periods of RSD?**
   - A) Improved coping strategies
   - B) Increased emotional resilience
   - C) Chronic emotional distress and potential depression
   - D) Enhanced self-confidence

1. **Which type of affirmations are beneficial during an RSD episode?**
   - A) Self-criticism
   - B) Validation of feelings
   - C) Denial of emotions
   - D) Blaming others

1. **How can journaling help someone with RSD?**
   - A) By worsening emotional pain
   - B) By providing a way to reflect and process emotions
   - C) By causing more confusion
   - D) By avoiding emotional issues

1. **Which of the following is a symptom of ADHD that overlaps with RSD?**
   - A) Sensitivity to rejection
   - B) Excessive planning
   - C) Inconsistent attention
   - D) High energy levels

1. **What type of feedback is most likely to trigger an RSD episode?**
   - A) Constructive feedback
   - B) Positive reinforcement
   - C) Neutral comments
   - D) Negative criticism

1. **How does RSD typically impact relationships?**
   - A) It strengthens relationships
   - B) It causes individuals to withdraw or react defensively
   - C) It improves communication
   - D) It has no impact on relationships

1. **Which strategy can help mitigate the impact of RSD?**
   - A) Avoiding all feedback
   - B) Practicing mindfulness and self-compassion
   - C) Ignoring emotional responses
   - D) Suppressing feelings

1. **What is the difference between RSD and general sensitivity to rejection?**
   - o A) RSD involves a chronic, intense emotional response, while general sensitivity is less severe
   - o B) General sensitivity is more intense than RSD
   - o C) RSD is unrelated to sensitivity to rejection
   - o D) RSD and general sensitivity are identical
1. **Which of the following is a recommended coping strategy for RSD?**
   - o A) Engaging in self-destructive behaviors
   - o B) Seeking professional therapy
   - o C) Ignoring emotional triggers
   - o D) Isolating oneself from others
1. **What is one of the key challenges in diagnosing RSD?**
   - o A) It is not recognized in formal diagnostic manuals
   - o B) It has clear, distinct symptoms
   - o C) It is easy to distinguish from other disorders
   - o D) It has a universal treatment protocol
1. **How can understanding one's personality traits help in managing RSD?**
   - o A) By increasing vulnerability to rejection

- B) By providing insights into personal triggers and emotional responses
- C) By making RSD symptoms worse
- D) By reducing self-awareness

1. **What is a common misconception about RSD?**
   - A) It is a rare condition
   - B) It only affects people with ADHD
   - C) It can be easily managed with willpower alone
   - D) It is not linked to emotional dysregulation

1. **Which of the following can be an effective long-term strategy for managing RSD?**
   - A) Avoiding all potential rejection
   - B) Developing a strong support network
   - C) Ignoring emotional needs
   - D) Relying solely on medication

1. **How can affirmations assist in building long-term self-acceptance?**
   - A) By reinforcing negative self-beliefs
   - B) By affirming positive aspects of oneself and challenging negative thoughts
   - C) By ignoring personal growth
   - D) By focusing only on external validation

1. **What is a typical emotional reaction during an RSD episode?**
   - A) Indifference
   - B) Euphoria
   - C) Overwhelming sadness or anger
   - D) Neutrality

1. **How can CBT (Cognitive Behavioral Therapy) help individuals with RSD?**
   - A) By reinforcing negative thought patterns
   - B) By challenging and modifying unhelpful thoughts and behaviors
   - C) By avoiding emotional issues
   - D) By focusing solely on medication

1. **What is a key feature of RSD that distinguishes it from other emotional responses?**
   - A) Its chronic and intense nature
   - B) Its short duration
   - C) Its lack of impact on self-esteem
   - D) Its minimal impact on daily life

1. **How can mindfulness practice benefit someone with RSD?**
   - A) By increasing emotional pain

- B) By helping individuals stay present and manage emotional reactions
- C) By causing more stress
- D) By avoiding self-awareness

1. **What role does self-compassion play in managing RSD?**
   - A) It increases feelings of inadequacy
   - B) It helps individuals be kinder to themselves during emotional distress
   - C) It has no impact on RSD
   - D) It worsens emotional pain

1. **How can journaling contribute to emotional healing from RSD?**
   - A) By intensifying emotional pain
   - B) By providing a safe space to express and process emotions
   - C) By creating more confusion
   - D) By avoiding emotional reflection

1. **Which of the following is NOT a symptom commonly associated with RSD?**
   - A) Severe emotional pain
   - B) Heightened sensitivity to rejection
   - C) Increased focus and productivity

- D) Defensive behavior

1. **What is a common emotional consequence of prolonged RSD episodes?**
   - A) Improved emotional resilience
   - B) Chronic sadness and potential depression
   - C) Enhanced self-confidence
   - D) Increased motivation

1. **How does RSD impact daily functioning?**
   - A) It enhances productivity
   - B) It often impairs daily tasks and responsibilities
   - C) It has no impact on daily activities
   - D) It improves organizational skills

1. **Which statement accurately describes the neurobiological aspect of RSD?**
   - A) RSD is purely a psychological phenomenon
   - B) RSD involves specific brain regions related to emotional processing
   - C) RSD is unrelated to brain function
   - D) RSD is a result of external factors alone

1. **What can be an effective method for someone with RSD to manage their emotional responses?**
   - A) Ignoring feelings
   - B) Using coping strategies and self-care practices

- C) Avoiding all social interactions
- D) Relying on medication alone

1. **What is one way to reduce the impact of RSD on relationships?**
   - A) By avoiding communication with others
   - B) By openly discussing feelings and seeking support
   - C) By withdrawing from social interactions
   - D) By suppressing emotions

1. **How can understanding personal triggers help in managing RSD?**
   - A) It has no impact on emotional responses
   - B) It allows for proactive management of emotional reactions
   - C) It worsens emotional distress
   - D) It eliminates the need for therapy

1. **Which of the following is NOT a common feature of ADHD?**
   - A) Impulsivity
   - B) Excessive self-doubt
   - C) Hyperfocus
   - D) High energy levels

1. **What role does therapy play in managing RSD?**

- A) It exacerbates RSD symptoms
- B) It provides tools and strategies for coping with emotional pain
- C) It has no impact on RSD
- D) It replaces the need for self-care

1. **How can individuals with RSD benefit from developing a strong support network?**
   - A) By increasing feelings of isolation
   - B) By providing emotional support and validation
   - C) By avoiding emotional issues
   - D) By reducing the need for therapy

1. **What is a recommended approach for someone experiencing chronic RSD?**
   - A) Ignoring emotional pain
   - B) Seeking professional help and developing coping strategies
   - C) Isolating oneself
   - D) Relying on self-diagnosis

1. **Which of the following is a key component of CBT for managing RSD?**
   - A) Avoiding challenging negative thoughts
   - B) Identifying and restructuring unhelpful thought patterns

- C) Focusing solely on medication
- D) Ignoring emotional triggers

1. **How can practicing self-care impact RSD?**
   - A) It increases emotional distress
   - B) It helps in managing stress and emotional pain
   - C) It has no impact on RSD
   - D) It worsens symptoms

1. **What is a common emotional experience for someone with RSD after a rejection?**
   - A) Indifference
   - B) Overwhelming sadness or anger
   - C) Euphoria
   - D) Calmness

1. **How does RSD typically affect self-perception?**
   - A) It enhances self-confidence
   - B) It can lead to feelings of inadequacy and self-doubt
   - C) It stabilizes self-esteem
   - D) It has no effect on self-perception

1. **What is a primary goal of therapy for RSD?**
   - A) To avoid all emotional pain
   - B) To provide tools for managing emotional responses and improving self-esteem

- C) To focus solely on medication
- D) To eliminate the need for self-reflection

1. **How can positive affirmations help someone with RSD?**
   - A) By reinforcing negative self-beliefs
   - B) By challenging and counteracting negative thoughts and promoting self-compassion
   - C) By ignoring personal growth
   - D) By focusing only on external validation

1. **What is an effective way to use journaling for managing RSD?**
   - A) By avoiding reflection on emotional experiences
   - B) By documenting and reflecting on emotional responses to understand triggers and patterns
   - C) By creating more confusion
   - D) By ignoring emotional pain

1. **How can mindfulness practice assist individuals with RSD?**
   - A) By increasing emotional pain
   - B) By helping individuals remain present and manage emotional reactions more effectively
   - C) By avoiding emotional issues

- D) By focusing solely on medication

1. **Which type of feedback is least likely to trigger RSD?**
   - A) Constructive criticism
   - B) Positive reinforcement
   - C) Neutral comments
   - D) Negative feedback

1. **What is a common misconception about RSD?**
   - A) It is a widely recognized and understood condition
   - B) It only affects people with ADHD
   - C) It is not linked to emotional dysregulation
   - D) It can be managed with willpower alone

1. **What is a recommended long-term strategy for managing RSD?**
   - A) Avoiding all potential rejection
   - B) Developing a strong support network and practicing self-care
   - C) Ignoring emotional triggers
   - D) Relying solely on medication

1. **What is the primary emotional impact of experiencing RSD episodes?**
   - A) Increased joy
   - B) Heightened self-confidence

- o C) Severe emotional distress and sadness
- o D) Neutral emotional state

1. **How can understanding RSD benefit individuals in managing their emotional responses?**
   - o A) By increasing emotional pain
   - o B) By providing insights into personal triggers and responses, allowing for better management
   - o C) By creating more confusion
   - o D) By avoiding self-awareness

1. **How can therapy help individuals with RSD?**
   - o A) By reinforcing negative thought patterns
   - o B) By providing strategies and tools for managing emotional pain and improving self-esteem
   - o C) By avoiding emotional triggers
   - o D) By focusing solely on medication

1. **What is a typical behavioral response during an RSD episode?**
   - o A) Enhanced productivity
   - o B) Withdrawal or defensive reactions
   - o C) Increased social interaction
   - o D) Overachievement

1. **What role does self-compassion play in managing RSD?**

- A) It increases feelings of inadequacy
- B) It helps individuals be kinder to themselves during emotional distress
- C) It has no impact on RSD
- D) It worsens emotional pain

1. **How can affirmations assist with long-term self-acceptance for individuals with RSD?**
   - A) By focusing on external validation
   - B) By affirming positive aspects of oneself and challenging negative thoughts
   - C) By ignoring personal growth
   - D) By reinforcing negative self-beliefs

1. **What is a key characteristic of RSD that distinguishes it from general emotional sensitivity?**
   - A) Its chronic and intense nature
   - B) Its short duration
   - C) Its minimal impact on daily life
   - D) Its lack of emotional pain

1. **How does mindfulness help in managing RSD?**
   - A) By increasing emotional pain
   - B) By helping individuals remain present and manage emotional reactions
   - C) By creating more stress

- o   D) By avoiding self-awareness

1. **What is a common outcome of chronic RSD episodes?**
   - o   A) Increased emotional resilience
   - o   B) Chronic sadness and potential depression
   - o   C) Enhanced self-confidence
   - o   D) Improved motivation

1. **Which of the following is NOT a recommended coping strategy for RSD?**
   - o   A) Engaging in self-care
   - o   B) Seeking professional therapy
   - o   C) Ignoring emotional triggers
   - o   D) Developing a strong support network

1. **How can journaling assist individuals with RSD?**
   - o   A) By intensifying emotional pain
   - o   B) By providing a safe space to express and reflect on emotions
   - o   C) By creating confusion
   - o   D) By avoiding emotional reflection

1. **What role does self-awareness play in managing RSD?**
   - o   A) It increases vulnerability to rejection

- B) It helps in recognizing and addressing emotional responses
- C) It worsens RSD symptoms
- D) It replaces the need for therapy

1. **Which therapeutic approach focuses on identifying and restructuring unhelpful thought patterns for RSD?**
    - A) Dialectical Behavior Therapy (DBT)
    - B) Cognitive Behavioral Therapy (CBT)
    - C) Art Therapy
    - D) Music Therapy

1. **What is a common emotional experience following an RSD episode?**
    - A) Overwhelming joy
    - B) Heightened sense of achievement
    - C) Intense self-doubt and sadness
    - D) Increased productivity

1. **What is one of the key challenges in diagnosing RSD?**
    - A) It is well-recognized and understood
    - B) It is not formally recognized in diagnostic manuals
    - C) It has clear and distinct symptoms
    - D) It has a universal treatment protocol

1. **How can understanding personal triggers aid in managing RSD?**
    - A) By increasing emotional distress
    - B) By allowing proactive management of emotional reactions
    - C) By worsening symptoms
    - D) By eliminating the need for therapy
1. **What is an effective long-term strategy for managing RSD?**
    - A) Avoiding all potential rejection
    - B) Developing coping strategies and a strong support network
    - C) Ignoring emotional pain
    - D) Relying solely on medication
1. **Which approach is recommended for someone with chronic RSD?**
    - A) Isolating oneself
    - B) Seeking professional help and developing coping strategies
    - C) Relying on self-diagnosis
    - D) Ignoring emotional triggers
1. **What is a key aspect of self-compassion in managing RSD?**

- A) It reinforces negative self-beliefs
- B) It involves being kind to oneself during times of emotional distress
- C) It has no impact on RSD
- D) It worsens self-esteem

1. **How can mindfulness practice assist in managing emotional responses for those with RSD?**
   - A) By increasing emotional pain
   - B) By helping individuals stay grounded and manage reactions more effectively
   - C) By creating more stress
   - D) By avoiding emotional issues

1. **What is a common outcome for someone experiencing repeated RSD episodes?**
   - A) Increased emotional resilience
   - B) Chronic sadness and potential depression
   - C) Improved motivation
   - D) Enhanced self-confidence

1. **What role does CBT play in managing RSD?**
   - A) It focuses on medication alone
   - B) It helps in identifying and changing negative thought patterns
   - C) It ignores emotional triggers

- o D) It reinforces negative thought patterns
1. **What is the impact of positive affirmations on RSD?**
    - o A) They reinforce negative self-beliefs
    - o B) They challenge negative thoughts and promote self-compassion
    - o C) They have no impact on emotional distress
    - o D) They focus on external validation
1. **Which of the following is NOT a recommended strategy for managing RSD?**
    - o A) Developing a strong support network
    - o B) Engaging in self-care activities
    - o C) Ignoring emotional triggers
    - o D) Seeking professional therapy
1. **What is an effective use of journaling for someone with RSD?**
    - o A) Creating confusion about emotional responses
    - o B) Documenting and reflecting on emotions to understand patterns and triggers
    - o C) Avoiding emotional reflection
    - o D) Ignoring emotional pain
1. **What is the primary focus of therapy for managing RSD?**
    - o A) To avoid all emotional pain

- B) To provide tools for managing emotional responses and improving self-esteem
- C) To focus solely on medication
- D) To eliminate the need for self-care

1. **How does RSD typically affect self-esteem?**
   - A) It enhances self-confidence
   - B) It can lead to feelings of inadequacy and self-doubt
   - C) It stabilizes self-esteem
   - D) It has no effect on self-esteem

1. **What is a key feature of RSD that differentiates it from general emotional sensitivity?**
   - A) Its brief and fleeting nature
   - B) Its chronic and intense nature
   - C) Its minimal impact on daily life
   - D) Its lack of emotional pain

1. **How can individuals with RSD benefit from developing self-awareness?**
   - A) By increasing emotional distress
   - B) By understanding personal triggers and managing responses more effectively
   - C) By worsening symptoms
   - D) By avoiding therapy

1. **Which type of feedback is most likely to trigger RSD?**
   - A) Positive reinforcement
   - B) Neutral comments
   - C) Constructive criticism
   - D) Negative feedback

1. **What is a common misconception about RSD?**
   - A) It is a recognized and well-understood condition
   - B) It only affects people with ADHD
   - C) It is linked to emotional dysregulation
   - D) It can be managed with willpower alone

1. **What is an effective long-term strategy for managing RSD?**
   - A) Avoiding potential rejection
   - B) Developing coping strategies and building a strong support network
   - C) Ignoring emotional triggers
   - D) Relying solely on medication

1. **What role does therapy play in managing RSD?**
   - A) It exacerbates symptoms
   - B) It provides strategies and tools for managing emotional responses and improving self-esteem
   - C) It focuses only on medication

- D) It ignores emotional triggers

1. **How can self-compassion assist individuals with RSD?**
    - A) By increasing feelings of inadequacy
    - B) By helping individuals be kinder to themselves during emotional distress
    - C) By worsening emotional pain
    - D) By ignoring personal growth

1. **What is a recommended approach for managing RSD triggers?**
    - A) Ignoring them
    - B) Understanding and proactively managing them
    - C) Avoiding self-reflection
    - D) Relying solely on medication

1. **What is the primary goal of self-care for individuals with RSD?**
    - A) To increase emotional pain
    - B) To manage stress and emotional pain more effectively
    - C) To focus solely on external validation
    - D) To ignore emotional triggers

1. **Which therapeutic approach is commonly used to address RSD?**

- A) Cognitive Behavioral Therapy (CBT)
- B) Music Therapy
- C) Art Therapy
- D) Dance Therapy

1. **What is a common emotional experience for someone with RSD after rejection?**
   - A) Overwhelming joy
   - B) Heightened sense of achievement
   - C) Intense sadness or anger
   - D) Increased motivation

1. **How can mindfulness practice benefit individuals with RSD?**
   - A) By increasing emotional pain
   - B) By helping individuals remain present and manage emotional reactions
   - C) By creating more stress
   - D) By avoiding emotional issues

1. **What is a key characteristic of RSD?**
   - A) Short and brief emotional episodes
   - B) Chronic and intense emotional pain
   - C) Minimal impact on daily life
   - D) Lack of emotional response

1. **What is an effective long-term strategy for managing RSD?**
   - A) Avoiding all potential rejection
   - B) Developing coping strategies and building a strong support network
   - C) Ignoring emotional pain
   - D) Relying solely on medication
1. **How does RSD affect self-esteem?**
   - A) It enhances self-confidence
   - B) It can lead to feelings of inadequacy and self-doubt
   - C) It stabilizes self-esteem
   - D) It has no effect on self-esteem
1. **What role does self-awareness play in managing RSD?**
   - A) It increases emotional pain
   - B) It helps in recognizing and addressing emotional responses
   - C) It worsens symptoms
   - D) It replaces the need for therapy
1. **Which approach is recommended for someone with chronic RSD?**
   - A) Ignoring emotional triggers

- B) Seeking professional help and developing coping strategies
- C) Isolating oneself
- D) Relying on self-diagnosis

1. **What is a common misconception about RSD?**
   - A) It is a well-recognized condition
   - B) It only affects individuals with ADHD
   - C) It is linked to emotional dysregulation
   - D) It can be managed with willpower alone

1. **How can journaling assist individuals with RSD?**
   - A) By increasing emotional distress
   - B) By providing a safe space to express and reflect on emotions
   - C) By creating confusion
   - D) By avoiding self-reflection

1. **What is a key aspect of self-compassion in managing RSD? -**
   - A) It increases feelings of inadequacy
   - B) involves being kind to oneself during emotional distress
   - C) It has no impact on RSD -
   - D) It worsens self-esteem

Answers:

1. B) Extreme emotional responses to perceived or actual rejection

2. B) Intense emotional pain following perceived or actual rejection
3. B) A significant sensitivity to criticism or rejection
4. B) Cognitive Behavioral Therapy (CBT)
5. B) Helping individuals understand and manage their emotional responses
6. B) By recognizing and addressing emotional triggers and patterns
7. B) By understanding and managing emotional responses
8. B) Managing emotional responses and developing coping strategies
9. B) Increased emotional sensitivity and pain
10. B) It can lead to extreme emotional responses, including anger or sadness
11. B) It helps individuals identify and manage emotional triggers
12. B) Negative or critical feedback
13. B) By recognizing and addressing unhelpful thought patterns
14. B) Rejection Sensitive Dysphoria (RSD)
15. B) By helping individuals remain present and manage emotional responses more effectively

16. B) By providing a safe space to express and reflect on emotions
17. B) To provide tools for managing emotional responses and improving self-esteem
18. B) By challenging and counteracting negative thoughts
19. B) It can lead to increased emotional distress and self-doubt
20. B) By providing tools and strategies for managing emotional pain
21. B) By helping individuals understand and manage their emotional responses
22. B) To develop coping strategies and improve emotional resilience
23. B) By documenting and reflecting on emotional responses to understand triggers
24. B) By understanding personal triggers and patterns, allowing for better management
25. B) By providing strategies for managing emotional responses and improving self-esteem
26. B) By understanding personal triggers and managing emotional responses

27. B) By helping individuals be kinder to themselves during emotional distress
28. B) By helping individuals stay grounded and manage reactions more effectively
29. B) By helping individuals remain present and manage their emotional responses
30. B) By helping individuals understand their emotional responses and manage them better
31. B) By helping individuals be kinder to themselves during emotional distress
32. B) By challenging negative thoughts and promoting self-compassion
33. B) By helping individuals stay grounded and manage their reactions more effectively
34. B) By developing coping strategies and building a strong support network
35. B) By helping individuals understand their emotional responses and manage them better
36. B) By helping individuals be kinder to themselves during emotional distress
37. B) By helping individuals stay grounded and manage their reactions more effectively

38. B) By providing tools and strategies for managing emotional responses and improving self-esteem

39. B) By developing coping strategies and building a strong support network

40. B) By recognizing and addressing negative thought patterns and providing coping strategies

41. B) By providing strategies for managing emotional responses and improving self-esteem

42. B) By helping individuals remain present and manage their emotional responses more effectively

43. B) By providing strategies for managing emotional responses and improving self-esteem

44. B) By helping individuals stay grounded and manage their emotional responses more effectively

45. B) By developing coping strategies and building a strong support network

46. B) By helping individuals understand their emotional responses and manage them better

47. B) By helping individuals be kinder to themselves during emotional distress

48. B) By helping individuals stay grounded and manage their reactions more effectively

49. B) By developing coping strategies and building a strong support network

50. B) By providing tools and strategies for managing emotional responses and improving self-esteem

51. B) By helping individuals stay grounded and manage their emotional responses more effectively

52. B) By developing coping strategies and building a strong support network

53. B) By helping individuals understand their emotional responses and manage them better

54. B) By developing coping strategies and building a strong support network

55. B) By providing tools and strategies for managing emotional responses and improving self-esteem

56. B) By developing coping strategies and building a strong support network

57. B) By helping individuals stay grounded and manage their reactions more effectively

58. B) By helping individuals be kinder to themselves during emotional distress

59. B) By providing tools and strategies for managing emotional responses and improving self-esteem

60. B) By helping individuals stay grounded and manage their reactions more effectively
61. B) By helping individuals understand their emotional responses and manage them better
62. B) By developing coping strategies and building a strong support network
63. B) By helping individuals be kinder to themselves during emotional distress
64. B) By providing tools and strategies for managing emotional responses and improving self-esteem
65. B) By helping individuals stay grounded and manage their reactions more effectively
66. B) By providing tools and strategies for managing emotional responses and improving self-esteem
67. B) By developing coping strategies and building a strong support network
68. B) By helping individuals understand their emotional responses and manage them better
69. B) By providing tools and strategies for managing emotional responses and improving self-esteem
70. B) By developing coping strategies and building a strong support network

71. B) By helping individuals stay grounded and manage their reactions more effectively
72. B) By helping individuals be kinder to themselves during emotional distress
73. B) By helping individuals stay grounded and manage reactions more effectively
74. B) Chronic sadness and potential depression
75. B) It helps in identifying and changing negative thought patterns
76. B) They challenge negative thoughts and promote self-compassion
77. C) Ignoring emotional triggers
78. B) Documenting and reflecting on emotions to understand patterns and triggers
79. B) To provide tools for managing emotional responses and improving self-esteem
80. B) It can lead to feelings of inadequacy and self-doubt
81. B) Its chronic and intense nature
82. B) By understanding personal triggers and managing responses more effectively
83. D) Negative feedback
84. D) It can be managed with willpower alone

85. B) Developing coping strategies and building a strong support network
86. B) It provides strategies and tools for managing emotional responses and improving self-esteem
87. B) By helping individuals be kinder to themselves during emotional distress
88. B) Understanding and proactively managing them
89. B) To manage stress and emotional pain more effectively
90. A) Cognitive Behavioral Therapy (CBT)
91. C) Intense sadness or anger
92. B) By helping individuals remain present and manage emotional reactions
93. B) Chronic and intense emotional pain
94. B) Developing coping strategies and building a strong support network
95. B) It can lead to feelings of inadequacy and self-doubt
96. B) It helps in recognizing and addressing emotional responses
97. B) Seeking professional help and developing coping strategies
98. D) It can be managed with willpower alone

99. B) By providing a safe space to express and reflect on emotions

100. B) It involves being kind to oneself during emotional distress

Made in the USA
Columbia, SC
04 February 2025

53270415R00172